The
Armenian Table

VICTORIA JENANYAN WISE is the author of fourteen cookbooks, including the bestselling *The Well-Filled Tortilla* (co-authored with Susanna Hoffman), *The Gardeners' Community Cookbook, The Pressure Cooker Gourmet* and, most recently, *Bold: A Cookbook of Big Flavors*. She lives in Oakland, California, with her husband, the cinematographer Rick Wise, who shot the food photographs for the cover of this book. Her website is www.wisekitchen.com

ALSO BY VICTORIA JENANYAN WISE

❖

American Charcuterie: Recipes from Pig-by-the-Tail
Foods of the World
The Vegetarian Table: Mexico
The Vegetarian Table: Japan
GardenHouse: Bringing the Outdoors In
The Gardeners' Community Cookbook
The Pressure Cooker Gourmet

WITH SUSANNA HOFFMAN

Good & Plenty
The Well-Filled Tortilla Cookbook
The Well-Filled Microwave Cookbook
The Olive and the Caper

WITH MARGRIT BIEVER MONDAVI
AND ANNIE ROBERTS

Annie and Margrit: Recipes and Stories
from the Robert Mondavi Kitchen

The Armenian Table

❖

165 Treasured Recipes that
Bring Together Ancient Flavors and
21st-Century Style

Victoria Jenanyan Wise

FOOD PHOTOGRAPHY BY RICK WISE

CLAIRVIEW

Clairview Books
Hillside House, The Square
Forest Row, RH18 5ES

www.clairviewbooks.com

Published by Clairview 2013

First published by St. Martin's Press, New York, in 2004

A catalogue record for this book is available from the British Library

ISBN 978 1 905570 70 6

Black-and-white photos from family archives
Interior design by Kathryn Parise
Cover by Morgan Creative featuring colour food photography by
Rick Wise. Food styling by Victoria Jenanyan Wise and Rick Wise

Printed and bound by Berforts Ltd., Herts.

For my mother, Wilma Ruth Bright Jenanyan,
and, in memoriam, my father, Henry Edmund Jenanyan.
Together,
they taught me the joy and security of sharing food
around a family table every day.
I am eternally grateful.

Contents

✤

Acknowledgments

❖

For me, cooking is a family affair, and, in my case, so is cookbook writing. I am blessed to have had the help and input of three special persons, without whose expertise and guidance this book would not be. I thank:

My husband, Rick Wise, ever avid when it comes to matters of food, as he is passionate about his profession, cinematography. He is the designated grill and sauté chef in our household, and the one who has fine-tuned the timing and turning for all the recipes that require such skill, as well as taken the beautiful food photographs that are included herein. Plus, natural storyteller that he is, he's had a hand in editing my sometimes amorphous side notes to make them cogent and "pan out."

My cousin Gary Jenanyan, who has perhaps the finest palate and taste memory on the planet. I have relied on him for details of our childhood dishes and stories, and had great good fun discussing and devising how we do it the same or differently today.

My dear friend over three decades, esteemed anthropologist, and sometimes cookbook coauthor Susanna Hoffman, who probably knows more about geography and peoples and their languages and foods than anyone in the world. She's always there to answer my questions about the difference between Near East, Middle East, and the modern semantics that have elided them, plus have a good laugh about how crazy life is as we cook up something new.

I thank also my cousin Bob White, for sharing remembrances and kindly trusting me with some of the precious family photos he has in his archive so they could be copied for this book; my sisters, Arayah Jenanyan, Beverly Bright Jenanyan, and Deborah Jenanyan Budrick, all partners in life, for the wonderful and poignant times we have had and continue to share; my son, Jenan Wise, light of my life and joy of my days, who is such a good team player at the family table, willing to focus on the dish and offer his comments as we dine upon a recipe, even as he would prefer to go dancing with his pals.

I thank my agents, Martha Casselman and Carole Bidnick, who believed in this book from the get-go and put lots of energy into getting it going; Judith Thomas, Martha's "right hand," who is always at hand to keep things sorted out and encourage me; and my editor at St. Martin's Press, Marian Lizzi, and her assistant, Julie Mente, who agreed this was a book that should be on your cookbook shelf and got it into publication.

Finally, I thank my Armenian heritage. It's one that is loving, intrepid, and cheerful through all. I feel lucky.

The Homelands of the Armenian People

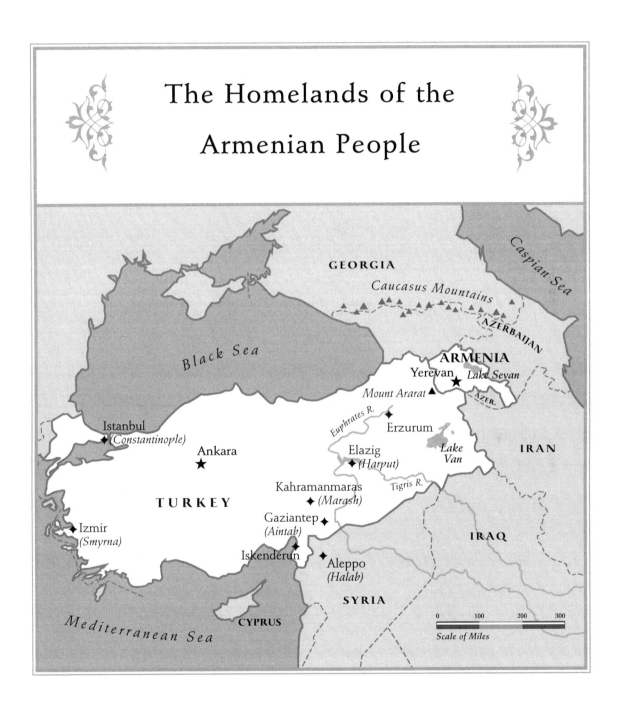

Introduction

THE ARMENIAN TABLE,
FROM ARARAT TO AMERICA AND ME

❖

In the first decade of the twentieth century, when the Ottoman Empire was collapsing and its leaders desperately needed a scapegoat, the Turkish Armenians became that scapegoat. The Armenian people had confronted similar situations many times over the centuries. Often, they had met such challenges and incursions by fighting and winning, sometimes by leaving to establish themselves on more welcome shores. In the years between 1912 and 1924, they had no choice but to move. They were overpowered, and, to escape massacre in Turkey, long one of their homelands, these oft-uprooted people came to America.

Virtually all Armenians in the United States today are here as a result of that emigration. Though some ended their journeys along the shores of the Mediterranean around Marseilles, Morocco, and Algeria, most pressed on to land at Ellis Island. From there, they dispersed to the greater Boston area, Chicago and its environs, and central and southern California on the West Coast.

Pioneers in keeping with the American spirit, these new immigrants brought the well-worn, sturdy baggage they had lugged across many

seas. In it were their portable possessions and a 4,000-year history full of memories, hopes, and energy.

Old as Sargon and the kingdom of Urartu before the Armenians as a nation or culture even existed, the baggage held the ghosts of Hskan, the first Armenian king in 600 B.C.E., and Tigranes IV, who in the fourth century A.D.E. led them to Christianity and away from the surrounding Assyrians and Persians who were about to embrace Islam. It held unfading images of the valleys and mountains of their homeland, from Mount Ararat, the Armenians' holy mountain where Noah docked his Ark during the biblical Great Flood, and south through the fertile Mesopotamian Valley to the Mediterranean. It held vivid memories of the grapes and walnuts and wheat and metal pots and elaborate hand-loomed rugs and weavings they had cultivated and fabricated for centuries but had to leave behind. Most of all, as with all exiled or expatriate people, it held the strongest pieces of the fabric of their culture that they could manifest wherever fate took them: their languages, their religion, their rituals, and, of course, their food.

❖

For me, the journey to this cookbook began with my Armenian grandparents, my father's parents, Victoria and Hatcher Jenanyan. They came from southern-central Turkey, where it shares a border with Syria. In the New World, along with other family members, they settled first outside Fresno in a small town called Yettem—really just a dot on the map—in California's Central Valley. What a shock! The cities of their childhoods had been Marash, Iskenderun, and Aintab, all of which were sophisticated and bustling cosmopolitan centers that had long included enclaves of educated Armenian entrepreneurs. The family spoke Turkish and Armenian in their homes, and they earned their living as professors, doctors, cobblers, and, yes, rug merchants. There were some especially erudite members who also spoke French, German, and some English as well.

In the New World, they wound up as grape farmers, until they lost their farms in the Great Depression. Some stayed in the Central Valley and switched crops to fruit such as peaches, nectarines, plums, and tomatoes. Others extended the Armenian diaspora north to the city of Sacramento to work in the thriving tomato canneries. My father's parents were among those who returned to an urban environment in Sacramento, and that's where the story picks up for me.

My mom and dad on their wedding day, March 13, 1944.

My father was the last-born child of Victoria and Hatcher, and the only one of their four children who was born in this country. At the outset of World War II, as a young man, he joined the United States military forces and became a pilot, and later, a bombardier. In 1943, he met my mother, Wilma Ruth Bright, in Albuquerque, New Mexico, her hometown, where he was stationed for flight training school. My mother, eighteen years old, was working in a photography shop when one day my father came in to pick up some photos of himself to send to his mother. It was love at first sight. Eight months later, they were married, and stayed passionately so for fifty-seven years, through thick and thin and the raising of their four daughters. I was the eldest.

After the war, my father was deployed to Japan to join the occupation forces there. He was flying observation flights, but when the Korean War started, he decided he'd had enough war stuff, so when he was asked to be in charge of the mess hall, he took the opportunity. He scouted out a local farm with chicken coops and gardens and began raising poultry and growing produce for the mess hall kitchen. My mother and I, now four and a half years old, along with my sister, Arayah, now two, soon joined him there. It is from those early days that I have the memory of my father involved in culinary matters, though that was not his ultimate path: He later chose finance and accounting as a career.

Through the years, our family moved to where the military sent us— Japan, Wisconsin, back to California, Hawaii, Omaha, Nebraska, and back to California again. As was normal in those days, my mother kept the house and cooked, feeding six of us—my younger sisters Beverly and Deborah having been born along the way—three times a day. We, including Dad, always went off to work and school with homemade bag lunches after a hearty breakfast at home, and looked forward to a well-rounded dinner at the end of the day. In Armenian style, our family focused on food, and being together for the preparation, serving, and partaking of it was how we came together through good times and bad.

Throughout our family peregrinations, we regularly visited the Sacramento relatives, who were the major family figures of my childhood in terms of food. Sometimes we stayed with them for long stretches—for instance, when my mother, sister Arayah, and I were awaiting the call to join my father in Japan. (That's when I took a notion to draw upon my grandmother's hand-stitched white coverlet with one of my mother's lipsticks. Probably the picture wasn't as estimable as the coverlet. Fortunately, all was forgiven, thanks to the generosity of my grandmother.)

Memorable among the elders were a patriarch and a matriarch, not married to each other but related by marriage on separate sides of the family. The patriarch was Hatcher's brother, my great uncle, Samuel Sarkis Jenanyan, known as "Uncle Doc" because he was a medical doctor in what was referred to as the Old Country and had attended medical school in Chicago to become certified in America. The matriarch was my eponymous grandmother, Victoria Jenanyan, known to the extended family as "Aunty Grandma." As heads of separate Jenanyan families, they were hosts, sometimes apart and sometimes together, for large family occasions.

Both Victoria and Uncle Doc had small, solid, tree-shaded white houses in Sacramento's working-class southside neighborhood. Both homes, each set on a verdant half-acre jammed full of fruit trees, were a child's garden of delight—fragrant, earthly paradises. There were peaches, plums, apricots, loquats, and figs—luscious Black Missions and plump, jammy Calimyrnas, as well as, in Uncle Doc's yard, a mulberry tree that rained its sweet, messy red fruit into the waiting hands of us children every summer. In the back of both properties were arbors covered with Thompson seedless grapevines whose tender leaves were used for wrapping delightful packages of rice and lamb mixtures called sarmas.

Every spring, Victoria and Uncle Doc each planted incredible vegetable gardens from which the families would eat for the whole summer, with plenty left over to put by for the winter months. It was a special thrill to have a jar of amber, bright orange, chartreuse, deep green, or red-tinged preserves opened and presented for a get-together meal, formal or informal. To this day, jars of my own put-by pickles and preserves, always in my pantry, reinforce and honor this food memory.

The ritual days spent with the Armenian relatives were noisy, full of people three generations strong, joyous, dramatic, spiced with melodrama, and replete with food. There was always someone to talk to, or to talk at you, even if you didn't particularly care for the conversation—isolation is not part of the Armenian culture. And it all happened around an abundant table.

❖

I am an inheritor of that conviviality—as one Armenian friend expressed it, "We like to eat together only a little more than we like to eat." I still cook Armenian food, and its flavors and scents permeate my cooking. Yet, I have had my own adventures and world travels. Through exposure to other influences, ingredients, and styles, I have been seduced by global flavors. As has happened with the descendants of so many other immigrant peoples in the United States, though grounded in the bedrock of a proud old culture, things have changed a bit. My menus feature the beloved, time-honored dishes and flavors of childhood, but these days the lamb might be served with mint vinaigrette or the chicken with a turmeric-colored yogurt sauce. I serve far more fish than was usual in my childhood because it is available and fits well with the traditional flavors I love. When I make Armenian pizzas, I often spread them with the adored traditional lamb mixture, but I might instead opt for a snappy topping of onion confit with toasted pecans or wilted leeks with Fontina cheese.

I think my Armenian elders would approve of such changes and innovations. After all, Armenian cooks have always been open to broadening their vocabulary of food ingredients and to improvising ingredient combinations when opportunity provided. From Persians they picked up the use of exotic spices such as cinnamon and cumin and the Eastern Mediterranean use of walnuts, pine nuts, and almonds as well as fruits, such as figs, pomegranates, quinces, and apricots, to season a dish. Flat breads—pita and lavosh—were adopted from the ancient peoples of the wheat-rich surrounding Caucasus area, as was the uninhibited use of fresh herbs—typically mint, dill, cilantro, and parsley. From the Turks, who probably learned it from the Greeks, Armenians adopted the techniques of using egg and lemon to thicken and brighten sauces for chicken and of cooking fish and vegetables plaki-style. Tourshi pickles of various vegetables, sesame candies, Turkish coffee, and more are all part of that heritage.

In my cooking, I continue that wide-open attitude, and in my dishes, I continue to expand the horizon with a plenitude of New World ingredients. In my life, I carry the metaphorical baggage of goods and flavors brought from Mount Ararat to me. Having them is a joy, not a burden. Here's a cookbook full of the old and the new as I savor Armenia.

The Armenian
Cupboard

❖

Throughout history, as they migrated from their lush homeland in the center of the spice route and on to new worlds, Armenian cooks have embraced new foods, integrating them into their daily fare to create a rich and varied cuisine. Tangy yogurt and cheeses, tart grape leaves and sharp pickled vegetables, a bevy of spices and fresh herbs, unctuous olive oil, nippy eggplant and Aleppo pepper, healthful grains for pilafs, nuts and dried fruits for savory as well as sweet dishes, all have long been cupboard staples. New basics, now so long assimilated it's hard to remember they weren't available until they were introduced from the New World in the sixteenth century, include essential produce: dried runner beans, green beans, bell peppers, potatoes, zucchini, pumpkin seeds for a favorite snack, and especially tomatoes, used every way— raw, cooked, stuffed, and stewed. Altogether, the cupboard holds a nutritious and fragrant mix, aromatic and colorful as a spice bazaar or open-air market. Following is a list of what to keep on hand. Most items are available in supermarkets and gourmet food boutiques. For the odd ingredients you might not find there, Near East, Middle Eastern, and

Mediterranean specialty stores can provide, or you can order online from www.kalustyans.com, whose import selections are top quality.

NUTS

Whole and ground, nuts are used and served from morning to night. Along with walnuts, which are the signature nut of Armenian cooking, always in the cupboard are almonds, pine nuts, and pistachios.

SEEDS

Sesame, one of the world's oldest seasonings, is used whole or ground to a paste as tahini; pumpkin seeds, from the New World, are toasted for a favorite snack or suspended in sweet brittles.

DRIED FRUITS

Dried apricots, the quintessential Armenian fruit, along with dried figs, dates, prunes, sour plums, and raisins, are used in all manner of ways, from a vegetablelike element in savory dishes to the centerpiece of sweet desserts.

HERBS

Most common are parsley, mint, cilantro, and dill, used fresh and profusely. In smaller quantities, frequently called-for herbs are bay, oregano, basil, savory, marjoram, thyme, and tarragon. These are usually used fresh, but sometimes dried as well. Rosemary and sage are practically unheard of in traditional Armenian cooking, but I say, herb away, and use them all.

SPICES

For a full Armenian cupboard of spices, keep the following on hand.

Salt—sea or kosher salt; the recipes in this book all call for kosher salt because it is the most readily available pure salt, but a fine-grained, not powdered, sea salt is the alternative of choice.

Black peppercorns—whole, so you can freshly grind them to retain the most of their berry flavor, aroma, and pleasing crunch.

Dried peppers—paprika, cayenne, and Aleppo pepper, named after the town of Aleppo in Syria where the finest quality comes from—these dried and ground capsicums are used as an alternative for or in addition to black pepper. Aleppo pepper, also known as Near East pepper, is the preferred one for Armenian cooking. It has a vegetably hot pepper taste that can be simulated, though not duplicated, with a mix of 1 tablespoon paprika and ⅛ teaspoon cayenne.

Daily spices—these include allspice, cumin, cinnamon, caraway, clove, coriander, nutmeg, saffron, and turmeric.

In addition, have on hand: fenugreek—chaiman in Armenian—key in making the spice mix called Chaiman Paste (page 44); and, especially for Turkish Armenian dishes, mahleb, the dried pits of black cherries, ground to season breads and cakes; nigella (black onion seed, sometimes called black caraway, which it doesn't taste like at all but resembles in appearance), for seasoning string cheese and sprinkling on savory breads and rolls; and sumac, the red berries of a nonpoisonous varietal of sumac shrub, for lending a lemony note to fish, meat, poultry, sauces, and marinades.

Fragrant Extracts

Orange flower water—used in syrups for soaking cakes and in a candy brittle of sesame seeds (page 290).

Rose water—used to flavor beef stews, meat kuftas, and especially, in this book, Walnut Brittle (page 291). This seasoning is beloved by Armenian cooks.

The Sour Element

Lemon juice and cider vinegar are the standard acid seasonings. I also employ red wine vinegar when I want a sharper acid taste, and balsamic vinegar for a woodsy acid flavor.

In addition, pomegranate syrup, the juice of sour pomegranates boiled down to achieve a molasses consistency, and verjuice, the liquid obtained from pressing sour unripe grapes, both provide a soft, fruity acid element to marinades and sauces. They should be stored in the refrigerator.

FATS

Olive oil—more used in Turkish Armenian cooking than in Caucasian Armenian cooking, where butter is often preferred, although in both branches of the cuisine olive oil is used when the dish is to be served cold, because it doesn't congeal. I always call for extra virgin olive oil. It doesn't need to be the ultra-expensive kind, just extra virgin, which means it's a first pressing with less than 1% acidity and therefore has no pithy taste.

Butter—Armenian cooks of old always clarified their butter to silt out the whey and thus make it more preservable (like ghee, of Indian cooking). While that's a delicious way to go, and does allow the butter to be kept longer, it requires more volume for less product. I skip the step and simply use stick butter, salted or unsalted, for daily cooking. When the difference between them affects the taste of the dish, I specify in the recipe.

Shortening and margarine—for some breads, like Lavosh (page 63), and cookies (page 269) where butter is too rich and olive oil is not binding enough, vegetable shortening or margarine is called for. For health and taste reasons both, I always use organic vegetable shortening with no transfats, and soy margarine because it's not too salty.

THE PRODUCE BIN

Alliums—onions, leeks, shallots, scallions, and garlic are used with abandon (although garlic is not as effusively used as it is in Greek, Italian, or California cooking).

Eggplants—an Old World staple, eggplant is a principal ingredient in Armenian cooking. With one or two on hand—they keep well in the refrigerator for 2 weeks or so—you can always whip up an Armenian dish.

Grape leaves—jarred or fresh, grape leaves are used to wrap sarmas, fish, and small birds; garnish pilafs, and mix into boerek fillings.

Green beans—although a New World crop, green beans are included in countless Armenian dishes from mazas to stews and braises.

Leafy greens—crunchy romaine and iceberg lettuces are used for salads; spinach is used for salads, fillings, soups, and stews; and cabbage, the only brassica besides cauliflower common in Armenian cooking, is used for salads, dolmas, and stews.

Fresh peppers—green bells, rather than the more currently popular red bells, are used for pickles, salads, dolmas, soups, and stews. Fresh chile peppers are not employed in Armenian cooking, though dried chile peppers are (see page 11)—but I take liberty here and always have a few jalapeños or serranos on hand.

Tomatoes—both fresh and canned tomatoes are a must-have for Armenian food. When fresh, they are sometimes sliced or diced without peeling; occasionally they are peeled and seeded. Store fresh tomatoes at room temperature to ripen and develop sweetness. Store opened canned ones in the refrigerator for up to 1 week or freeze for up to 3 months. Also, keep a good-quality, unseasoned tomato paste to enrich dishes when fresh tomatoes are not at their peak of ripeness and flavor.

In addition, have on hand standard produce staples: potatoes, carrots, and celery for soups, stews, casseroles, and other dishes.

PEELING AND SEEDING TOMATOES

Plunge the tomatoes into boiling water for 10 seconds. Drain and set aside to cool enough to handle. Slip off the skins with your fingers. Cut the tomatoes in half crosswise and gently squeeze out the seeds into a colander set over a bowl. Use the tomatoes right away, along with the juices, if called for. Or, store the tomatoes and juices together in the refrigerator for up to 5 days, or freeze for up to 6 weeks.

GRAINS AND LEGUMES

Bulgur—bulgur is cooked, then dried, hurled (or threshed), and cracked wheat. It comes in three sizes—fine, medium, and coarse. It's nice to have all three because not just any bulgur will do for a particular recipe. For kufta, fine bulgur is the choice to achieve the lightest texture. Pilafs require a medium or coarse grind so the granules absorb the liquid and remain fluffy without becoming soggy. For tabbouli, medium grind is called for because it soaks to suppleness without any cooking.

Whole wheat berries—uncooked, threshed wheat berries, called dzedzadz in Armenian, are used in soups, stews, and the ancient sweet, Tarkana (page 293). Pearl barley can substitute in soups and stews; coarse bulgur can substitute in tarkana.

Rice—Armenians always use long grain white rice. I prefer the basmati varietal for its nutty flavor and fragrance, which befits Armenian dishes and adds extra presence over the more common California, Texas, or Carolina long grain rice.

Lentils—I use the small French green lentils because they hold their shape in cooking.

Chickpeas—also called garbanzo beans, chickpeas are an essential Old World legume. They are used whole to round out soups, stews, and salads, or can be roasted for a snack (page 35). Pureed, they are turned into kuftas and fritters (pages 125 and 127) and the world-renowned dip, Hummus (page 53). I heartily recommend buying dried chickpeas and cooking them at home (page 35): the ready-cooked canned ones don't have the same legumy taste.

CHICKEN BROTH

Armenian cooking features light-broth flavoring rather than the long-simmered, hearty stock flavoring of European cooking. If ready-made chicken broth is called for, I always make my own because it's fresher and cleaner tasting. If you are not so inclined, Swanson's low-sodium chicken broth is an acceptable substitute.

HOMEMADE CHICKEN BROTH

Homemade chicken broth will keep in the refrigerator sealed under its layer of fat for up to 2 weeks. Or, you can freeze it for up to 3 months.

Makes 2 quarts

> 3 pounds chicken pieces, such as wing tips, back-
>   bones, and gizzards
> 1 medium carrot, coarsely chopped
> 1 small yellow or white onion, halved
> 1 small rib celery, coarsely chopped
> 6 sprigs fresh flat-leaf parsley
> 2 sprigs fresh thyme or ¼ teaspoon dried thyme
> 10 cups water

Combine the ingredients in a large pot and bring to a boil over medium-high heat. Decrease the heat to maintain a simmer, and, without letting the liquid boil again, cook uncovered for 1½ hours, skimming from time to time. (The skimming ensures a clear broth.)

Strain the broth into a bowl, discarding the solids, and let cool completely. When cool, skim the fat off the top and proceed with the recipe. Or, to store, transfer the broth with its fat (the fat acts as a sealant) to a storage container and refrigerate for up to two weeks, or freeze longer. Remove the solidified fat from the top before using.

Yogurt: Essential and Versatile

❖

Yogurt, with its clean, tangy taste and smooth consistency, has lent itself to dishes from the eastern Mediterranean, north into the Caucasus, east through Afghanistan, and south to India since the time of Genghis Khan. In recent times, yogurt has moved from a relatively unknown food outside those regions to being embraced by the French as a snack food (Yoplait) and from there, into the mainstream of American healthy cooking. Yogurt was always in my culinary vocabulary—we called it by its Armenian name, madzoon—and it was a staple side sauce, sometimes plain, sometimes with cucumbers, always served alongside pilaf and other Armenian dishes my mother prepared. When I established my own household, I began to delve further into yogurt's possibilities. I discovered it can substitute in almost any recipe that calls for milk, buttermilk, sour cream, or crème fraîche. It is especially delightful used to impart a refreshing taste to cooked sauces, to thicken soups, or to serve as the base for sweets, such as Yogurt Panna Cotta (page 285). In this chapter, you will find yogurt basics, along with a collection of recipes based on my yogurt explorations.

Basic Yogurt
Madzoon

Making a large batch of yogurt was a regular affair in the kitchens of my mother, and of my Armenian grandmother and aunts. The process was so routine that it was done at least twice a week. That was a different era. Today, there are excellent, homemade-tasting commercial yogurts available even in supermarkets, and I rely on them as a time-saving alternative. Still, I offer the recipe, as my mother taught it to me, in case you'd like to try your hand at yogurt making.

Makes 2 quarts

2 quarts 2% milk (see box, page 19)
¼ cup starter yogurt, at room temperature, or
    one 10-gram pack powdered yogurt starter

Place the milk in a large, heavy enamel or nonstick saucepan over medium to medium-low heat. Bring to just below the boiling point, 180°F. This will take about 50 minutes, maybe a little more, depending on the size of the pot. Remove from the heat and set aside to cool to lukewarm (100°F), 40 to 45 minutes.

Lift the skin off the top of the milk (I use my fingers) and discard it. In a large bowl, whisk together the starter and 1 cup of the lukewarm milk, then slowly whisk in the remaining lukewarm milk from the pot. Cover first with plastic wrap, then with a towel large enough to wrap around the bowl. Set aside at room temperature until the yogurt is set to a soft custard consistency, at least 6 hours. Refrigerate to chill and firm for at least 3 hours. Will keep fresh-tasting for up to 2 weeks.

YOGURT KNOW-HOW

Yogurt can be made from any cow, sheep, or goat milk, nonfat to whole. I prefer 2% cows' milk because it results in a soft custard consistency with just the right balance between sharp and creamy flavors.

As important, the taste of the yogurt is also determined by the starter (called magart). I've tried making yogurt using a good-quality, commercial organic yogurt as starter; oddly, sometimes it works, and sometimes not, but always without as full a flavor as the original. It's better to begin with a powdered yogurt starter, available in health food stores.

It's important to bring the milk to the boiling point very slowly; otherwise, it will scorch on the bottom (not good for the flavor), and the pan will be a real chore to clean.

The time it takes for the yogurt to set is determined by the weather; in warm weather it reaches the desired custard consistency more quickly than in cool weather.

Once going, be sure to save out ½ cup from each batch of yogurt to make the next batch.

Yogurt Drink

Tan

Tan is the preferred beverage to accompany an Armenian meal or snack. Nothing more than yogurt thinned with water, seasoned with salt, and served over ice cubes (perhaps with the refinement of a mint sprig garnish or cucumber spear), it is refreshing—and a delicious way to enjoy the health benefits of calcium.

Makes one drink

¾ cup yogurt

¼ teaspoon kosher salt, or to taste

¾ to 1 cup water

Ice cubes, for serving

1 mint sprig (optional), for serving

1 cucumber spear (optional), for serving

Whisk together the yogurt, salt, and enough of the water to make the desired thinness. Half fill a tall glass with ice cubes and pour the tan into the glass. Garnish with the mint, if using, and serve.

Yogurt with Cucumber
Jajik

Jajik is the pervasive yogurt and cucumber side dish–cum–sauce served throughout the Eastern Mediterranean and Caucasus. My grandmother, Victoria Jenanyan, always added a few ice cubes as she served it. In my family, garlic or herbs were never in the jajik, but I often season the dish with a touch of mint because I like the sweet note it imparts, and because my son, Jenan, likes it that way.

Serves 4 to 6

2 cups yogurt
1 teaspoon kosher salt, or to taste
2 teaspoons chopped fresh mint (optional)
1 medium cucumber

Place the yogurt, salt, and mint, if using, in a bowl and whisk to smooth. Peel the cucumber, cut it in half lengthwise, and remove the seeds if they are large. Thinly slice the cucumber, pat the slices dry on paper towels, and stir into the yogurt. Chill before serving. Or, add several ice cubes to the bowl and serve right away (the jajik will be thinner this way).

Yogurt with Spinach

Yogurt with spinach can be served as an appetizer with cracker bread (lavosh) or pita bread, or as a side dish with pilafs. It is also especially good as a topping for grilled or broiled tomato halves. For the spinach, frozen won't do, and it doesn't need to: fresh spinach is widely available and takes but a moment to prepare. Baby spinach leaves, now also widely available, are great for salads, but for cooking I purchase bunched spinach—it gives more flavor when cooked and is doubly economical because the root ends can be wilted separately and used to garnish pilafs or stirred into stews.

Makes about 2 cups

> 1½ cups yogurt, drained for 30 minutes (page 24)
> 1 large bunch spinach, leaves and tender stems, finely
>   chopped (4 packed cups)
> 1 clove garlic
> ½ teaspoon kosher salt

Wash the spinach, drain it, and transfer while still moist to a large pot or microwave dish. Cover and cook on medium heat on the stove top or on high in the microwave until completely wilted but still bright green, about 5 minutes on the stove top or 3 minutes in the microwave. Drain in a colander and set aside to cool.

Place the drained yogurt in a bowl. Mince the garlic together with the salt and add it to the yogurt. Squeeze the spinach to remove any remaining liquid and add it to the yogurt. Mix with a fork, distributing the spinach throughout. Cover and place in the refrigerator to chill for at least 1 hour before serving.

VARIATIONS

❖ For a fancier Armenian version, sometimes served for Easter, stir in 1 tablespoon chopped fresh mint or dill and ¼ cup chopped fresh flat-leaf parsley.

❖ Add a Turkish touch with 1 teaspoon ground cumin stirred into the yogurt, along with the spinach.

❖ Take the dish in an Indian direction: warm 1 teaspoon yellow mustard seeds in 2 tablespoons olive oil over medium heat until the seeds begin to pop, 1 to 2 minutes. Pour over the chilled yogurt and spinach just before serving.

Drained Yogurt
All the Way to Cheese

For yogurt-based appetizers, side dishes, and sauces, the yogurt is first drained of its whey to achieve a thicker consistency and denser flavor in the dish. When left to drain overnight or longer, the yogurt becomes cheeselike and can be spread on bread or rolled into balls and marinated (page 50). Following are the guidelines for those various stages.

DRAINED YOGURT

1 quart yogurt

↬ Makes about
3 cups

Line a colander with a double layer of cheesecloth, making sure to have a generous drape over the sides. Set the colander in a bowl that holds its bottom well above the bottom of the bowl. Place the yogurt in the colander and set aside at room temperature to drain until reduced to 3 cups, 2 to 4 hours, depending on the consistency of the yogurt to begin with. Use right away, or store in the refrigerator for up to 1 week.

YOGURT CHEESE

2 cups drained yogurt (see preceding recipe)
1 teaspoon kosher salt

↬ Makes about
1 cup

Stir the salt into the drained yogurt in the colander. Cover and refrigerate to continue draining. Leave for 12 hours (overnight) to achieve a cream cheese texture. Leave for 24 hours to achieve a firmer, chèvrelike texture. Be sure to pour off the whey accumulated in the bowl whenever it reaches up to the bottom of the colander.

To serve yogurt cream cheese, dish it into a bowl and accompany with olives and pita or cracker bread. Will keep in the refrigerator for up to 1 week.

To serve firmer yogurt cheese, see page 50.

Armenian Crème Fraîche

With yogurt as the catalyst, sweet cream thickens into a nippy crème fraîche. Use it as you would sour cream to sauce Cabbage Sarmas (page 243) or Poppy Seed Cake (page 279).

Makes 2 cups

  2 cups heavy cream
  1 tablespoon yogurt

Whisk together the cream and yogurt in a bowl until smooth and well mixed. Cover with plastic wrap and set aside at room temperature for 24 to 48 hours, depending on the weather, until very thick like crème fraîche. Use right away, or store in the refrigerator for up to 2 weeks.

Yogurt Béchamel

*Béchamel, or white sauce, is a base for many classic European, Eastern Mediter-
ranean, and American dishes. Though out of the ordinary, making béchamel with
yogurt instead of milk situates it squarely within Armenian cooking, and it's an innovation I've turned to as my favorite. You can use it as a base for sauces to go on
fish, poultry, and vegetables; to enrich soups; to layer in lasagna and vegetable
gratins (Armenian Moussaka, page 148); to bind fillings (Chard Leaf Sarmas,
page 246); or to nap warm, open-face sandwiches of chicken or chipped beef. I always make béchamel in the microwave because it's a virtually fail-safe method,
which is why I've listed it first.*

Makes about
1⅔ cups

  3 tablespoons butter
  3 tablespoons all-purpose flour
  1½ cups yogurt, stirred to smooth
  ¼ teaspoon kosher salt
  Pinch of freshly ground nutmeg

To cook in the microwave: Place the butter in a large bowl and microwave
uncovered on high for 2 minutes, until foaming. Remove and whisk in the
flour. Return to the microwave and cook uncovered on high until boiling,
1 to 2 minutes. Remove, whisk in the yogurt, and microwave uncovered
on high for 2 minutes. Remove again, whisk to smooth, and continue microwaving uncovered on high until thickened, about 1 minute. Stir in the
salt and nutmeg, if using.

  To cook on the stove top: Melt the butter in a medium saucepan over
medium-high heat until foaming. Whisk in the flour, decrease the heat to

medium, and continue whisking until the mixture begins to turn golden, about 2 minutes. Add the yogurt and salt, whisk to smooth, and cook, stirring frequently, until thickened and creamy, 12 to 15 minutes more. Stir in the salt and nutmeg, if using.

Whether cooked in the microwave or on the stove top, the béchamel may be used right away. Or, cool, cover, and refrigerate for up to 1 week. When ready to serve, reheat in the microwave or on the stove top.

Yogurt and Barley Soup with Mint, Parsley, and Egg
Tanabour

Light yet satisfying, tanabour is a centuries-old Armenian comfort food enjoyed at breakfast, lunch, or dinner. A version with wheat berries, rather than pearl barley, is also typical (see Variations). The carrot is not typical, but I add it for color.

Serves 4 to 5

4 tablespoons butter
1 small yellow or white onion, finely chopped
½ cup pearl barley
4 cups low-sodium chicken broth
1 teaspoon kosher salt
1 small carrot, peeled and cut into ¼-inch dice
1½ cups Drained Yogurt (page 24)
1 large egg
2 teaspoons chopped fresh mint leaves
1 tablespoon chopped fresh flat-leaf parsley
Freshly ground black pepper

Melt 2 tablespoons of the butter in a large pot or pressure cooker over medium heat. Add the onions and cook until well wilted, 5 minutes. Add the barley and stir to mix and coat the grains. Add the broth and salt.

To cook on the stove top, bring to a boil over high heat. Decrease the heat to medium-low, cover, and cook for 50 minutes, until the barley is tender.

To pressure-cook, lock on the lid and bring to pressure over high heat, about 6 minutes. Decrease the heat to medium and cook for 20 minutes. Remove from the heat and let sit for 5 minutes. Gently release any remaining pressure and remove the lid.

Either way, add the carrot to the pot and continue cooking, uncovered, at a simmer until the carrot is tender, about 10 minutes.

Meanwhile, in a bowl, whisk together the yogurt and egg. Set aside. Melt the remaining 2 tablespoons butter in a small sauté pan over medium-high heat. Stir in the mint and parsley, immediately remove from the heat, and set aside in a warm place.

When the carrots are done, stir the yogurt mixture into the soup. If necessary, gently reheat without allowing to boil. Ladle into bowls, drizzle some herb butter over the top, and garnish with black pepper. Serve right away.

VARIATIONS

In place of the pearl barley, you can also use:

❖ Whole wheat berries (available in natural food stores and grocery markets that carry bulk grains). The cooking time, either on the stove top or in the pressure cooker, is the same as for pearl barley.

❖ Rice. Use 1 cup long grain white rice and cook on the stove top rather than the pressure cooker. Simmer for only 25 minutes before adding the carrots.

Yogurt, Potato, and Celery Soup

Serves 4

On blustery, cold Saturdays, my mother would whip up a soup like this for our family lunch. I've always loved her sublime inspiration of adding celery to potato soup. It's a repeat performance in my kitchen, except now I add an Armenian touch with yogurt, rather than a milk roux, for the thickening and enrichment.

> 3 russet potatoes, peeled and cut into 1-inch chunks
> 1 leek, trimmed, halved, thinly sliced, and washed
> 3 ribs celery, trimmed and thinly sliced
> 6 cups low-sodium chicken broth
> 1 large sprig thyme
> 2 teaspoons kosher salt
> 2 cups yogurt
> 1 tablespoon chopped fresh chives, for garnish

Place the potatoes, leek, celery, broth, thyme, and salt in a large, heavy pot and bring to a boil over medium-high heat. Decrease the heat to medium and cook until the potatoes are very tender and mashable, about 20 minutes. Remove the thyme sprig and set aside to cool for 10 minutes.

In a bowl, whisk the yogurt until smooth. Slowly add 2 cups of the slightly cooled soup, continuing to whisk to break up the potato pieces. Set aside.

Using the whisk, mash the potatoes in the pot until the mixture is somewhat smooth but still chunky. Return the pot to the burner over medium heat and reheat until beginning to boil. Whisk in the yogurt mixture and serve right away, garnished with the chives.

The Armenian
Maza Table

❖

Unlike many other highly social cultures of the world, Armenians don't
have much of a street culture. Instead of gathering at the village square,
in tavernas, and at sidewalk tables partaking of maza, appetizer and
snack foods, they're more inclined to "have people over," whether it be
at home, the church, a community hall, or a grand family reunion in a
park. For such celebratory occasions, they have developed a large reper-
toire of maza to spread on the table as people come together to meet
and greet off the street. And what a glorious display the Armenian maza
table is, offering the full spectrum of flavors—sour, salty, bitter, and
sweet—as well as the spectrum of food textures from crunchy to soft to
chewy. This chapter presents a host of Armenian savory maza offerings. For more, see the chapters on breads and savory pastries, salads,
"meat" balls, and sweets.

Toasted Pumpkin Seed, Roasted Chickpea, and Pistachio Nut Snacks
Chackerdack

Makes about 1½ cups

A bowl of crunchy morsels, onomatopoetically named chackerdack (the Armenian name for pumpkin seeds), is an ever-present snack in Armenian households. I happily continue the tradition. Not only is chackerdack a tasty treat, it staves off hunger that might otherwise lead you to less healthful junk food snacks! You can mix the pumpkin seeds with the chickpeas and pistachio nuts (purchased already toasted and salted), or, as I prefer, serve each in separate bowls.

Unhulled raw pumpkin seeds are usually used for chackerdack, but hulled seeds are much quicker to toast, and easier to eat. Hulled raw pumpkin seeds are available in health food stores, Latino markets, and grocery stores that have bulk bins.

TOASTED PUMPKIN SEEDS

> 1½ cups hulled raw pumpkin seeds
> Extra virgin olive oil, for toasting
> Kosher salt

Lightly grease a heavy (preferably cast iron) skillet or sauté pan large enough to hold the pumpkin seeds in one dense layer. Set it over medium-high heat until beginning to smoke. Add the pumpkin seeds, sprinkle lightly with salt, and cook over medium to medium-high heat, stirring frequently, until plump, toasted through, and no longer green-tasting, about 5 minutes. Cool slightly and serve. Will keep in an open bowl for up to 2 weeks.

ROASTED CHICKPEAS

1½ cups dried chickpeas
4 to 6 cups water
Extra virgin olive oil, for roasting
Kosher salt

Makes about
3½ cups

Place the chickpeas in a pressure cooker with 4 cups water or in a heavy pot with 6 cups water.

To pressure cook: Lock on the lid and bring to pressure over high heat, about 7 minutes. Cook on medium heat for 15 minutes. Remove from the heat and let sit for 15 minutes. Gently release any remaining pressure and remove the lid.

To cook on the stove top: Bring to a boil over high heat, cover, and cook on medium heat until tender, about 1 hour.

Either way, when done, drain the chickpeas, spread them on paper towels, and let sit for 30 minutes to dry out a bit.

To roast the chickpeas, preheat the oven to 325°F. Lightly grease a baking sheet with olive oil. Place the chickpeas on the baking sheet and roll them around to coat all over. Roast until slightly golden and crisp, 40 to 45 minutes. Sprinkle lightly with salt and serve, or store in an airtight container for up to 2 weeks.

Green Bell Pepper Pickle
Tourshi

Makes 2 quarts

Pickled vegetables of one sort or another accompany almost every Armenian meal. Green bell pepper tourshi and cucumber Gheteh (page 38) were especially popular in my family and were always served with softened cracker bread as appetizers for even the most casual of get-togethers. The brine can be more or less vinegary, more or less salty, with or without garlic and red chili pepper for seasoning, all depending on the cook's taste. Of all my Armenian relatives, Aunt Queenie, my father's sister-in-law, made my favorite tourshi, green bell peppers crisp to the bite, with a taste perfectly balanced between vinegar and salt. Here's the recipe as she taught it to my mother and my mother to me, except I like to spike the brine with garlic and red chili pepper.

Note: You can also seal the jars in a hot water bath for storing in the pantry. This is the way it was done when I was growing up because large quantities—too much to fit in the fridge without taking up all the space—were made at a time. I prefer to make a smaller batch and keep a modest jar or two in the refrigerator. No canning required.

4 medium green bell peppers, quartered, stemmed and
    membranes removed

2 cloves garlic, halved (optional)

1 small fresh or dried red chile pepper, halved lengthwise
    (optional)

2¼ cups cider vinegar

2¼ cups water

6 tablespoons kosher salt

Pack the bell pepper quarters in two 1-quart jars. Tuck 2 garlic halves and half a red chile pepper in each jar.

Combine the vinegar, water, and salt in a saucepan and bring to a boil over high heat. Stir to mix in and dissolve the salt, then remove from the heat. Cool slightly and pour over the peppers in the jars, filling all the way to the top. Cool completely, several hours, then cap and set aside at room temperature overnight. Store in the refrigerator to cure for at least 2 weeks before using. Will keep in the refrigerator indefinitely.

My godparents, Uncle Bob Jennings, my dad's brother, and Aunt Queenie, Bob's wife, in a glamour shot taken in their Sacramento garden, circa 1946.

OTHER VEGETABLES TO PICKLE

This brine also works for cauliflower, young green beans or haricots verts, and okra. With cauliflower, I include ½-inch-thick carrot ovals for color; for green beans, I omit the chili pepper; and for okra, I include a few sprigs of fresh dill.

Armenian Pickled Cucumbers
Gheteh

This recipe and narrative were written by my father when I requested he put down on paper his special cucumber pickle recipe for the Smith & Hawken Gardeners' Community Cookbook I was writing. His words and sidebar comments about the seeds and growing of Armenian cucumbers in the New World explain it all. I give the recipe as he taught it to me and quote his advice and reminiscences in the box below. Pale green, ridged-skin, curved Armenian cucumbers are available in produce stores and farmers' markets. Japanese, Persian, or small Kirby pickling cucumbers are good substitutes.

Makes 4 pints

6 cups scrubbed and sliced Armenian cucumbers
(½ inch thick)
4 cloves garlic
4 large sprigs dill
3 cups distilled white vinegar
1 cup water
⅓ cup kosher salt

Pack the cucumbers into four 1-pint jars. Place 1 clove of garlic and 1 dill sprig in each jar. Set aside while preparing the brine.

Combine the vinegar, water, and salt in a saucepan and stir to mix. Bring to a boil over medium-high heat. Pour over the cucumbers. Set the jars aside to cool completely. When cool, cap the jars, place in the refrigerator, and let rest for 2 weeks before using. Will keep up to 4 months in the refrigerator.

A CUCUMBER PICKLE STORY
BY MY FATHER, HENRY JENANYAN

"My family were merchants, not farmers, in the Old World (for us, that was Turkey). In the New World of California, the garden became a way to keep the treasured foods of our heritage. In apron-sized backyards, we grew tomatoes, peppers, eggplants, grapes, and cucumbers. These plants, many in their native New World environment, thrived and gave us produce for our beloved dishes. But the cucumbers, in the variety we prized, were not known in this new region. Their seeds, carried in pockets and pouches across many borders, were planted here. The seeds had to be collected at the end of each growing season so that there would be more for next year. The Armenian cucumbers, which we called gheteh, yielded the fruit for our favorite tourshi. Its small-seeded, tender-skinned produce were without rival. And so, as I moved here and there in my career as a military officer, I always kept a packet of Armenian cucumber seeds to plant wherever my next garden was, just as my immigrant parents had. Eventually, my wife took over the pickle making. Together, we passed the recipe on to our four daughters and share it here."

Green Tomato Pickle

Makes 4 quarts

My father's second favorite tourshi was green tomato pickle. Every October, from the end-of-season green tomatoes left on my husband Rick's luscious vines, too late to ripen, I would make a few jars for Dad's end-of-November birthday and our family's Thanksgiving. And I still do.

> 4 pounds green tomatoes, stemmed, rinsed, and cut
>   into 1-inch wedges
> 12 large sprigs dill
> 4 garlic cloves, sliced
> 3 cups distilled white vinegar
> 5 cups water
> ¼ cup kosher salt
> 8 whole cloves

Pack the tomatoes, dill sprigs, and garlic in four 1-quart jars.

Mix the vinegar, water, salt, and cloves in a large pot and bring to a boil over high heat. Pour over the tomatoes, filling the jars to the top. Set aside to cool completely, then cover and refrigerate for 5 days before using. Will keep in the refrigerator for up to 1 year.

Pearl Onion and Zucchini Tourshi in Sweetened Brine

To pickle pearl onions and zucchini, I use a mild, not too salty brine sweetened with sugar and made aromatic with whole cloves. It's an Armenian tourshi variation reminiscent of bread-and-butter pickles.

Makes 3 pints

3 cups pearl onions

2 medium zucchini, cut into ½-inch-thick rounds

2 cups cider vinegar

1 cup water

1 tablespoon kosher salt

2 tablespoons sugar

4 whole cloves

Peel the onions with a paring knife and pack them into 3 pint-size jars. Add the zucchini to each jar.

Combine the vinegar, water, salt, sugar, and cloves in a saucepan and bring to a boil over high heat. Pour into the jars, filling to the top, and set aside to cool completely. Cap and refrigerate for 1 week before using. Will keep in the refrigerator for up to 6 months.

Salted Turnips and Radishes with Scallions and Soft Cracker Bread

Serves 6

As all Armenians do, my father loved turnips. He would simply peel them (or not, if they were young enough), slice them into wedges, and serve them with just a sprinkle of salt. I added the radishes years later, for color, and also the scallions because their verdant nip is a good finishing touch to this fresh composition of brassica roots. Served with softened cracker bread and butter, it's reminiscent of the classic French dish of radishes with brown bread and butter.

3 smallish turnips (about ¾ pound)

1 bunch radishes

Kosher salt, for seasoning and for serving

2 scallions, white and light green part, cut lengthwise
　　into thin slivers

Armenian Cracker Bread, softened (page 64)

Best quality, creamery-style unsalted butter, at room
　　temperature, for serving

Peel the turnips and cut them lengthwise into thin wedges. Trim the radishes, leaving a few of the tiny, tender green leaves at the top, and cut them in half lengthwise. Arrange the turnip wedges and radish halves on a platter and sprinkle them lightly with salt. Strew the scallion slivers over the top. Serve with the cracker bread and butter on the side, with an additional small bowl of salt, in case someone would like a touch more.

Mock Basterma

Basterma, or pasterma, is the dried beef cold cut of Armenian cuisine. The old process included salting the beef and then air-drying it in a cool, breezy place for several weeks. I call my recipe mock basterma because the spice rub, untypically, includes sugar and brandy, and because the meat is cured in the refrigerator rather than air-dried. The result is a divine cold cut with the texture and suppleness of prosciutto, not too salty, and very easy to make.

Note: The only hard part of this recipe is that, to make the slices thin like prosciutto, the basterma really should be cut on a butcher's meat slicer. The good news is that I have found that butchers are willing to provide this service, usually without charge.

⁀ Makes 1 to
1½ pounds

⅔ cup coarse sea salt

⅔ cup sugar

3 tablespoons brandy or whiskey

⅓ cup Chaiman Paste (see page 44)

1½ to 2 pounds beef eye of round, trimmed of excess fat

Combine the salt, sugar, and brandy in a large deep dish. Rub the chaiman all over the beef. Add beef to the dish and turn to coat all around with the salt mixture. Cover with plastic wrap and set a weight, such as a large can of tomatoes, on top. Place in the refrigerator to cure for 4 to 5 days, turning once a day.

On the fourth or fifth day, rinse off the beef, pat it dry, and wrap in plastic wrap. Set aside in the refrigerator for 4 more days, or up to 4 weeks.

When ready to use, take the basterma to the butcher to slice thinly, as for prosciutto. The slices will keep wrapped in plastic wrap for up to 2 weeks. Or, freeze for up to 2 months.

CHAIMAN PASTE

Chaiman is the Armenian name both for fenugreek and for a paste made of fenu-greek with paprika and other spices. It's best known as a seasoning for basterma, but I find it a delightful topping or accompaniment for many other dishes, such as Potato and Chickpea Fritters (page 127). You can make up a batch and keep it in the refrigerator for weeks; it will thicken as it sits, so thin it with a little water before using.

Makes about ⅓ cup

1½ tablespoons ground fenugreek
1½ tablespoons mild paprika
½ teaspoon cayenne
½ teaspoon ground allspice
1 teaspoon ground cumin
1 teaspoon freshly ground black pepper
1 teaspoon kosher salt
⅓ cup water, or more, as needed

Combine all the ingredients in a bowl and stir with a fork to mix. Use right away or store in the refrigerator for up to several weeks, thinning with a little water, if necessary, before using.

Salted Cheese

Salting cheese to preserve it through winter, when the sheep and cows weren't producing milk for fresh cheese, is a very old story. I suspect the practice led to a taste for salted cheese, and so it continues as a treat of the Armenian table. The salting renders out the whey, creating a brine that preserves the cheese. Store salted cheese out of the refrigerator, at room or cellar temperature (48° to 65°F).

> 1 pound Muenster cheese, cut into 2-inch squares
>   about 1 inch thick
> ⅓ cup kosher salt

Place the cheese in a dish large enough to hold the pieces in one layer. Add the salt and turn to coat on all sides. Cover with plastic wrap and set aside at room temperature, turning once a day, for 5 days. After that, turn once every third day for 4 weeks. By then, there should be enough rendered liquid to come halfway up the cheese chunks. The cheese may be eaten at this point or kept for up to 3 months longer.

To serve, rinse the cheese cubes and soak in water for 15 minutes. Cut into smaller cubes or slices and serve with softened cracker bread and olives. Or, use the cheese rinsed but not soaked, like an Italian grana cheese, grated over gratins, pasta dishes, or salads.

String Cheese

String cheese is particularly Armenian. I have fond memories of staring into the pot with the cheese and water, waiting for just the right moment to retrieve the cheese when it was softened but still intact, before it had melted into oblivion. I offer the technique here because homemade string cheese is far superior to the bland vacuum-packed variety found in supermarkets, and because the fun of stretching and twisting the cheese once it's melted makes for terrific entertainment for children.

A good white melting cheese is all that's needed. In our family, it was made from Monterey jack or Muenster cheese because that's what was available in Sacramento in those days. Now, with the advent of excellent neighborhood cheese stores and Middle Eastern grocers, I suggest using the Old World cheese Tooma, which is similar in taste and texture, but has more flavor.

> ½ pound good white melting cheese, such as Monterey
>   jack, Muenster, or Tooma, cut into 2-inch squares
>   about 1 inch thick
> ¼ cup water
> 1 teaspoon nigella seeds (optional)

Place the cheese and water in a medium saucepan and bring to a boil over medium heat. Cook until the cheese is beginning to melt, about 5 minutes. Stir and add the nigella seeds, if using. Continue cooking for 5 minutes, until no longer lumpy. Drain in a colander, set the colander over the saucepan, and set aside until cool enough to handle, but still quite warm, 4 to 5 minutes.

Lift the cheese out of the colander and pull it into a length about 18 inches long, pinching it together when it starts to pull apart. Fold in half, squeeze together, and repeat the process two more times, each time winding up with a slightly shorter length. On the third round, twist the cheese into a "braid" about 6 inches long. Use right away, or wrap in plastic wrap and store in the refrigerator for up to several weeks.

Homemade Fresh Cheese

Fresh cheese means cheese that is not aged, like cottage cheese, farmer's cheese, and ricotta. Though these are traditionally made without salt, I prefer a pinch or two to enhance the cheese with saline flavor. The choice between whole milk and half-and-half cream is a matter of butterfat content. Of course, the more butterfat, the richer the cheese. It's important to let the cheese drain only as long as instructed: If left too long, you will have too dry a curd.

Makes about 2 cups (10 to 12 ounces) cheese

> 2 quarts whole milk or half-and-half cream
> ¼ cup distilled white vinegar
> 1 teaspoon kosher salt
> Armenian Cracker Bread (page 63) or other crackers and
>   Zesty Marinated Olives (page 51), for serving

Place the milk in a large, heavy saucepan over medium heat. Bring almost to a boil, 30 to 35 minutes (as in making yogurt; a skin will form over the top, but don't remove it).

Remove from the heat and stir in the vinegar (the milk will curdle) and salt. Let steep in the pot for 2 minutes, then pour the mixture into a colander lined with a double layer of cheesecloth and set over a bowl. Let sit for 1 hour at room temperature.

Lift up the cheesecloth, and gently squeeze out some of the liquid, leaving the cheese quite moist. Replace the cheese, still in the cheesecloth, in the colander over the bowl and set a weight on top. Let sit for another 30 minutes, until compacted but still moist.

Remove the cheesecloth, transfer the cheese to a clean bowl, cover, and refrigerate for 1 hour. Use right away or store in the refrigerator for up to 1 week.

Serve with cracker bread or other crackers and Zesty Marinated Olives as a maza. Or, use in boerek pastries (pages 77 and 83) or any dish that calls for savory cream cheese.

Yogurt Cheese Balls Marinated in Garlic Dill Oil with Aleppo Pepper

Serves 6 to 8

This is one of my favorite appetizer/maza dishes. Guests delight in its exotic yet familiar taste. To make it even prettier, when I have chives in blossom, I sprinkle some of their lavender flowers over the top along with the chives.

As well as serving the balls as an appetizer on their own, you can use them to garnish either of the Armenian tomato salads (pages 90 and 91) or Black-Eyed Pea Salad (page 92).

> 2 cups (2 batches) Yogurt Cheese (page 24)
> 6 tablespoons extra virgin olive oil
> 2 cloves garlic, pressed
> 2 teaspoons chopped fresh dill
> 1 teaspoon Aleppo pepper
> 1 tablespoon chopped fresh chives
> Armenian Cracker Bread (page 63) or other crackers,
>   for serving

Divide the cheese into 13 portions and roll each into a walnut-size ball. Set the balls, without touching, on a plate lined with paper towels. Cover loosely with paper towels and refrigerate for 4 to 6 hours, until firm.

In a small bowl, mix together the olive oil, garlic, dill, and Aleppo pepper. Transfer the balls to a deep dish or a high-lipped platter, all in one layer. Pour the oil mixture over the balls, cover loosely with plastic wrap, and refrigerate for 2 hours, or up to 1 week.

To serve, sprinkle the chives over the top and accompany with cracker bread or other crackers.

Zesty Marinated Olives

A bowl of olives is always welcome on the snack table; a bowl of marinated olives is even better. Be sure to use quality olives with pits. They work better because they absorb the seasonings without becoming oversoaked, and chewing the olive meat off the pit is half the fun of this internationally beloved snack. Remember to provide a bowl for the pits when serving.

Makes 7 cups

1 cup whole blanched almonds

2 teaspoons extra virgin olive oil

6 cups mixed good-quality olives, such as picholines and
    Kalamatas, not pitted

3 tablespoons finely chopped lemon zest

1 teaspoon fennel seed

1 large clove garlic, coarsely chopped

1 small fresh red chile pepper, stemmed, seeded, and
    slivered lengthwise

1 teaspoon freshly ground black pepper

1/4 cup red wine vinegar

1/4 cup extra virgin olive oil

Place the 2 teaspoons olive oil and almonds in a heavy skillet over medium-high heat. Cook, stirring, until the nuts are toasted, about 2 minutes. Set aside to cool.

In a large bowl, combine all the remaining ingredients, along with the toasted almonds, and stir to mix. Refrigerate to marinate for at least 24 hours. Will keep in the refrigerator for up to 2 weeks.

Green Olive and Walnut Relish

Like a tapenade, only coarser, this Armenian version of an olive relish is often served on the maza table to accompany softened Lavosh (page 63). You can also use it as a relish to dollop on simply grilled chicken or lamb skewers, or to roll up into Aram Sandwiches (page 65).

Makes 2 cups

1 cup mild green olives, such as Atalanti or picholines
⅓ cup finely chopped yellow or white onion
⅓ packed cup whole fresh flat-leaf parsley leaves
⅓ cup coarsely chopped walnuts
2 teaspoons finely chopped fresh lemon zest
½ teaspoon Aleppo pepper
2 tablespoons freshly squeezed lemon juice
1 tablespoon extra virgin olive oil

Spread the olives on a counter and, with a mallet or hammer, tap each one hard enough to break it open without cracking the pit. Remove the pits with your fingers and coarsely chop the olives. Place the olives in a bowl, add the remaining ingredients, and toss to mix. Serve right away or refrigerate for up to 1 week.

Chickpea Tahini Dip

Hummus

Ubiquitous on snack tables throughout the Middle East and now routinely offered in American delis, hummus can be served as a dip or as an accompaniment to grilled meats, chicken, and eggplant. For authentic, and best, flavor, you should start with dried chickpeas and cook them yourself rather than using canned, already cooked ones.

Makes
2½ cups

1 cup cooked chickpeas (page 35), cooking liquid
    reserved
3 cloves garlic, pressed
⅓ cup freshly squeezed lemon juice
¼ cup tahini paste
½ cup extra virgin olive oil
1 teaspoon kosher salt
Toasted pita triangles (page 68), for serving

In a food processor, puree together the chickpeas, garlic, lemon juice, tahini, olive oil, and salt. Add enough of the cooking liquid, ⅓ to ½ cup, to make a creamy, loose consistency. Serve with the pita triangles on the side for dipping. Will keep in the refrigerator for up to 1 week.

Eggplant Salad Dip

I first learned this recipe not from my family, but from my dear friend and sometime coauthor Susanna Hoffman, who learned it in Greece when she was doing field study work in anthropology. Together, and with friends, we made a veritable vat of it for Rick's and my wedding, and went on to offer up many more vats at our art student café, The Good & Plenty, on the campus of the California College of Arts and Crafts in Oakland, California. I offer the recipe here in a home amount so you can enjoy it for smaller-party occasions. The vegetables and herbs should be well chopped but not minced, to keep the salady nature of the dish.

Serves 6 to 8

1 large eggplant (about 1½ pounds)

¼ yellow or white onion, chopped

2 large cloves garlic, finely chopped

1 small ripe red tomato, chopped

2 tablespoons chopped fresh flat-leaf parsley

½ teaspoon chopped fresh mint leaves

½ teaspoon chopped fresh oregano leaves

⅛ teaspoon dry mustard or ½ teaspoon prepared
    Dijon-style mustard

1½ tablespoons red wine vinegar

1½ teaspoons freshly squeezed lemon juice

¼ cup extra virgin olive oil

½ teaspoon kosher salt

¼ teaspoon freshly ground black pepper

Pita (page 68), softened Armenian Cracker Bread
    (page 63), or baguette slices, for serving

Preheat the oven to 450°F. Prick the eggplant once with a knife, place it on a baking sheet, and roast in the oven until the eggplant collapses under wrinkled skin, about 50 minutes. Remove and let cool enough to handle.

Slit the eggplant open lengthwise and scoop the pulp into a bowl. Add the remaining ingredients, except the bread, and mash with a fork to mix and break up the eggplant. Set aside at room temperature for 30 minutes for the flavors to marry, or refrigerate for up to 3 days.

Serve in a bowl with a basket of breads on the side.

Stuffed Baby Eggplants
Imam Bayildi

Serves 12

Imam bayildi appears as maza in the Middle East, throughout the Mediter-ranean, and on American-Armenian tables from Boston to Chicago to Glendale. It remains basically the same from pillar to post, with a few minor changes. Armeni-ans like to include a little green bell pepper in the stuffing. I like that touch, and the recipe here includes it. Small, elongated, narrow eggplants are preferred for imam bayildi. They are available in Asian, Italian, and Middle Eastern markets as well as produce stores and supermarkets that carry a multiethnic selection of vegetables.

6 small Japanese or Italian eggplants (about 3 ounces each)
⅓ cup extra virgin olive oil
1 medium yellow or white onion, finely chopped
6 large cloves garlic, finely chopped
1 medium green bell pepper, finely chopped
1½ teaspoons kosher salt
¾ teaspoon freshly ground black pepper
1 medium tomato, finely chopped
¼ cup chopped fresh flat-leaf parsley
2 tablespoons whole fresh flat-leaf parsley leaves,
    for garnish

To prepare the eggplants, cut off the stem ends and cut the eggplants in half lengthwise. Scoop out some of the pulp from each half (a grapefruit spoon works well), chop it, and set aside.

Heat half of the olive oil in a large sauté pan over medium-high heat. Add the eggplant shells, cut sides down, and sauté, pressing them down once or twice, until golden. Turn the shells over and continue cooking on medium heat until browned on the other side, about 1 minute more. Transfer the shells, cut sides up, to a baking dish large enough to hold them in one tightly packed layer. Set aside.

Preheat the oven to 350°F.

Add the remaining olive oil to the pan, along with the eggplant pulp, onion, garlic, bell pepper, salt, and black pepper. Stir to mix and sauté on medium to medium-high heat until the mixture is collapsing and the vegetables are quite soft, about 5 minutes. Stir in the tomato and chopped parsley and continue cooking over medium heat until most of the liquid evaporates, about 5 minutes more.

Spoon the mixture into the eggplant shells in the baking dish. Pour enough water around, not into, the shells to come ¼ inch up the sides of the dish. Bake for 30 minutes, until the shells are very soft and the stuffing is bubbling. Remove and cool to room temperature.

Cover the dish and refrigerate until thoroughly chilled—overnight is best, up to 3 days is okay.

To serve, transfer the eggplants to a platter and sprinkle with the parsley leaves.

Breads and Savory Pastries

❖

Located on a high plateau between the southern Caucasus Mountains and northern Iran, the original Armenian homeland was a perfect site for growing wheat. Indeed, it was perhaps the birthplace of wheat agriculture. In ancient times, it, along with barley, was an essential source of carbohydrate for a huge population that did not yet have corn, rice, or any legumes besides fava beans, chickpeas, and lentils. Culinarily, wheat, a gift of nature refined by human cultivation, has been exploited in Armenian cooking in numerous wonderful ways, from bulgur pilafs to breads, savory and sweet pastries and puddings, and more. Here is a roster of breads and savory pastries, served from morning to dinnertime, that I think of as an extension of the Armenian maza table.

Coffee Rolls
Choeregs

Choeregs are sweet yeast rolls a little bit like cakey bagels served at breakfast or with coffee or tea in the afternoon. At either time, choeregs are suited to taking in a sweet direction with an accompaniment of Green Fig and Fennel Seed Marmalade (page 61) or in a savory direction, with a topping of smoked salmon and a squeeze of lemon juice. Best of all, serve them both ways for a festive brunch.

Makes
14 rolls

1 package active dry yeast

¼ cup warm water

3 cups all-purpose flour, plus extra for kneading

¾ teaspoon baking powder

½ teaspoon kosher salt

½ cup (1 stick) butter, melted and cooled

½ cup lukewarm milk

2 large eggs

¼ cup sugar

2 teaspoons ground mahleb or 2 tablespoons ground
   dried mulberries (see box, page 62)

Olive oil, for coating the dough ball

1 egg, beaten, for glazing the rolls

¼ cup sesame seeds, for topping the rolls

Place the yeast in a large bowl and sprinkle the warm water over it. Let sit for 5 minutes, until bubbly. Sift together the flour, baking powder, and salt and set aside.

Add the butter, milk, eggs, sugar, and mahleb or mulberry to the bowl with the yeast and beat with a wire whisk or electric mixer until well blended. Gradually beat in the flour mixture in 1 cup amounts, until you have a medium-soft dough that's still a little scraggly. With your hands, knead the dough in the bowl for a minute or two, adding extra flour, up to ⅓ cup, until smooth and cohesive. Gather into a ball, coat with oil, and return to the bowl. Cover and set aside in a warm place to rise until doubled in bulk, 1½ to 2 hours.

Punch down the dough and divide it into 14 portions. Pat each portion into a smooth ball. Flatten each ball between your palms into a 3-inch disk and poke a hole in the center, so it looks like a small bagel. Place on ungreased baking sheets 3 inches apart. Cover with dry cloths and set aside in a warm place to rise again until doubled in bulk, 1 to 1½ hours.

To cook the rolls, preheat the oven to 350°F. Glaze the top of each with the beaten egg and sprinkle each with about 1 teaspoon sesame seeds. Bake until golden and a knife inserted in the center comes out clean, 15 to 20 minutes. Remove and let cool on the baking sheets.

Serve while slightly warm. Or, cool completely and store in plastic bags at room temperature for up to 3 days, or freeze for up to 2 months.

GREEN FIG AND FENNEL SEED MARMALADE

This marmalade is an excellent condiment to have on hand for spreading on breakfast toast or coffee rolls or topping ice cream. It also makes an unusual accompaniment for kebabs of pork, lamb, or chicken. And it's a snap to make in a microwave oven.

Makes 3 cups

> 2 pounds fresh, firm green figs
> 1½ cups sugar
> ¼ teaspoon fennel seed
> 2 tablespoons freshly squeezed lemon juice

Cut the figs into quarters and place them in a large microwave bowl. Add the sugar, stir to mix, cover, and set aside to macerate overnight.

Next day, add the fennel seed and stir to mix. Microwave on high for 5 minutes, until beginning to boil. Stir and continue microwaving on high for 10 minutes, until bubbling. Stir again and continue microwaving for 5 minutes, until the liquid is bubbling almost to the top of the bowl. Remove and stir in the lemon juice. Set aside until cool, then chill overnight before using. Will keep up to 3 months or longer in the refrigerator.

ABOUT CHOEREG AND DRIED MULBERRIES

Typically, mahleb, with its bitter cherry taste, or anise seed flavors choereg rolls. I often opt instead for ground dried mulberries (a member of the fig family, Moraceae) because I like its unique, dulcet tone with a hint of malt, like an old-fashioned malted milk shake. Mulberries grow on trees that are planted primarily for their leaves to feed silkworms. The berries, when fresh, have an intensely sweet flavor with almost no hint of acid. When dried, they are soft and can be chewed to snack upon, as the Turks do, or mixed with ground walnuts for a kind of trail mix, called chakida, as the Afghanis do. Or, they can easily be ground in a food processor and used to flavor choereg and other breads and pastries. Dried mulberries can be ordered from www.kalustyans.com.

Armenian Cracker Bread
Lavosh

Makes six 12-to-13-inch rounds

Lavosh is a yeast dough cracker bread specific to Armenian cuisine. The large rounds are served crisp, like a cracker, for dipping into Green Olive and Walnut Relish (page 52), Eggplant Salad Dip (page 54), or Hummus (page 53). Softened to make it more breadlike, it accompanies pickles, olives, cheese, and other hors d'oeuvres or is rolled into Aram Sandwiches (page 65).

Dry cracker bread is not easy to find outside metropolitan areas that have Middle Eastern grocery stores, but the dough for cracker bread is easy to knead and roll out, requiring no extra flour, and I highly recommend you make your own. Pre-softened cracker bread is more readily available, but it has no flavor. Dry cracker bread will keep for weeks in a paper bag at room temperature.

Note: Instead of the more traditional sesame seeds, you can top the lavosh with caraway seeds (my favorite), cumin seeds, nigella seeds, or flax seeds.

1 package active dry yeast

1 cup warm water

4 tablespoons (½ stick) margarine or organic vegetable
    shortening, melted and cooled

1½ teaspoons sugar

2½ teaspoons kosher salt

3½ cups all-purpose flour

Extra virgin olive oil, for coating the dough ball

1 tablespoon sesame seeds or other seeds
    (see Note, above)

In a large bowl, dissolve the yeast in the water. Let sit 10 minutes, until bubbly. Add the margarine or shortening, sugar, salt, and flour. Mix and knead in the bowl until the dough can be gathered into a ball, then knead on a counter until smooth and elastic, about 6 minutes. Coat lightly with olive oil, return to the bowl, and let rise until doubled in bulk, about 1½ hours—up to 2½ hours is okay.

Punch down the dough and divide it into 6 balls. Let sit for 15 minutes. Preheat the oven to 400°F.

Roll out each ball into a 12- to 13-inch round. As you do this, sprinkle each round all across the top with water, then with some of the seeds. Pass the rolling pin over the top 2 more times to press in the seeds and keep them from popping off as the bread cooks. Place on individual baking sheets and bake until bubbled up and golden in spots, about 8 minutes. Serve warm, at room temperature, or softened (see below).

HOW TO SOFTEN LAVOSH

To soften lavosh, dampen the cracker on both sides by moistening it under tap water. Shake off the excess water and wrap the bread in damp kitchen towels. Place in a plastic bag, such as a small plastic garbage bag. Set aside for 45 minutes to 1 hour, until soft enough to tear into pieces. Or, for Aram Sandwiches (page 65), let sit for 2 hours, until soft enough to roll up without tearing.

Aram Sandwiches

When softened, Armenian cracker bread is supple enough to use as a wrap for sandwiches. Aram sandwiches, as they have come to be called, invite artful combinations of meats, vegetables, and cheeses. When sliced, they look like colorful pinwheels, as pretty to behold as they are light and tasty to eat. Following are three favorite compositions that always "flew out the door" at my Pig-by-the-Tail delicatessen—where we made many, many each day for the lunch crowd and many more for party trays—plus a list of further suggestions.

Makes 1 roll, serves 1 to 2 for lunch or 3 to 4 as maza

1 round Armenian Cracker Bread, softened
(page 63)
Extra virgin olive oil

Hard-Boiled Egg and Anchovy Filling

1 packed cup baby arugula leaves
2 large eggs, hard-boiled (page 195) and chopped
4 anchovy fillets, chopped
1 tablespoon capers, drained
8 to 10 thin slices ripe tomato
Kosher salt and freshly ground black pepper, to taste

❖

Recipe continues on next page

Cucumber and Watercress Filling

      1 packed cup watercress, leaves and tender top stems
      ½ medium Armenian or English cucumber, thinly
            sliced
      8 to 10 thin slices ripe tomato
      Kosher salt, to taste
      2½ ounces feta cheese, crumbled

Tomato, Onion, and Chopped Olive Filling

      6 large leaves red leaf or butter lettuce
      8 thin slices Monterey jack, Muenster, or fontina
            cheese
      3 thinly sliced white or red onion rings, separated
      8 to 10 thin slices ripe tomato
      ⅓ cup chopped Kalamata olives

To make the Aram sandwich, lightly coat the softened bread with olive oil. Layer on the ingredients for the filling you are using in the order given in the filling ingredient list. Roll up and slice crosswise into 4 to 6 rounds, depending on whether serving for lunch sandwiches or as maza.

    Serve right away or wrap in plastic wrap and set aside at room temperature for up to 3 hours before serving.

OTHER FANCIFUL FILLINGS FOR ARAM SANDWICHES

Armenian Ratatouille (page 227)

Mock Basterma (page 43) with Green Bell Pepper Pickle (page 36)

Thinly sliced roast beef with lettuce, onion rings, and cornichons

BLT-style, with bacon, lettuce, and tomato

Ham, cheese, and lettuce; heat in the microwave or toaster oven before serving

Fried Eggplant (page 216) with pressed garlic and lettuce

Sautéed and vinegar-deglazed radicchio shreds with black pepper and feta cheese

Homemade Pita Bread

Yeast flat breads, from lavosh and lahmajoun to pizza and pita, have long been used as edible plates for holding and wrapping other foods. Pita bread is so basic and so widespread, its popularity has remained as constant as its name—a name that, with Greek influence, became the root of both pie and pizza. It's so simple to make that I encourage you to try your hand at it.

Note: For a more rustic pita, use half white flour and half whole-wheat flour.

Makes twelve 8- to 9-inch pita breads

    2 cups warm water
    1 teaspoon sugar
    2 packages active dry yeast
    6 cups all-purpose flour, plus extra for rolling out
        the dough
    2 teaspoons kosher salt
    ⅓ cup extra virgin olive oil, plus extra for coating
        the dough ball

Stir together one cup of the water and the sugar in a small bowl. Sprinkle the yeast over the top and set aside for 15 minutes, until bubbly.

Place the flour and salt in a large mixing bowl. Make a well in the center and pour in the oil, yeast mixture, and remaining 1 cup water. Stir with a wooden spoon until crumbly, then knead in the bowl until the dough can be scooped into a ball. Transfer to a counter and knead until smooth and elastic, about 5 minutes. Lightly coat the dough ball with oil, return to the bowl, and set aside in a warm place to rise until doubled in bulk, about 1½ hours.

Punch down the dough and let it rest for 20 minutes (it will start to rise again).

Divide the dough into 12 equal portions. On a lightly floured surface, roll out each portion to make an 8- to 9-inch circle about ⅛ inch thick. Set the dough circles aside, without stacking them, and cover with a damp cloth so they don't dry out. Let rest for 30 minutes (a little longer is okay).

While the dough rests, preheat the oven to 500°F.

When ready to bake, place as many dough circles as will fit on a baking sheet without overlapping. Bake for 3 minutes, until puffed up. Check the oven and rotate the baking sheets if the pitas are baking unevenly. Continue baking for 2 minutes more, until the pitas are beginning to turn golden on the bottom but are not at all crispy. Remove and set aside to cool slightly. Continue with another batch until the pitas are cooked.

The pitas may be served right away. Or, cool completely and store in plastic bags at room temperature for up to 5 days.

Armenian Pizza
Lahmajoun

Makes sixteen 6-inch thin pizzas or ten thicker ones

Lahmajoun is special fare, a gift from the cook to family and guests for weddings and high holidays. There's no doubt that making them, though not difficult, requires a bit of time and care. The crust is similar to that of standard pizza except the dough is given a second, brief rising before cooking. In my family, the dough was rolled out thin to make a crackerlike crust and the pizzas were served open face. Another traditional style has the dough rolled out thicker to make a softer crust, somewhere between a deep-dish pizza crust and pita bread, and folded over for eating. The basic dough recipe is the same, and the lahmajouns are delicious both ways.

Dough

    1 package active dry yeast

    3 tablespoons warm water

    ¾ cup lukewarm water

    1 teaspoon sugar

    1 teaspoon kosher salt

    3 tablespoons extra virgin olive oil, plus extra for
        coating the dough ball

    2½ cups all-purpose flour

    Extra water and/or flour, if necessary

Pizzas

Flour, for rolling out the dough

Traditional Lamb Topping, Wilted Leek and Fontina Cheese
Topping, Onion Confit and Pecan Topping, or Aintab-
Style Eggplant, Tomato, and Green Bell Pepper Topping
(recipes follow, pages 73–76)

To make the dough, in a large mixing bowl, stir together the yeast and
warm water. Set aside for 15 minutes, until bubbly.

Stir in the lukewarm water, sugar, salt, and oil. Sift in the flour and
blend, adding a little more flour or water if necessary to make a dough
that you can gather into a ball. On a floured surface, knead the dough until it is elastic and shiny but still soft, about 8 minutes. Lightly coat the
dough ball with olive oil and return to the bowl. Cover with a towel and
set aside in a warm place until doubled in volume, 1½ to 2 hours. Punch
down the dough and use it right away, or wrap it in plastic wrap and refrigerate for up to 2 days (bring to room temperature before rolling out).

To make the pizzas, place the dough on a well-floured surface and cut
it into portions, 10 if making thicker pizzas, 16 for thinner ones. Roll each
portion between the palms of your hands to form a small ball. Roll the
balls in flour to coat and cover them first with a well-rung-out damp
towel and then a dry towel. Let rest for at least 15 minutes, up to 1 hour.

Preheat the oven to 475°F.

On a lightly floured surface, roll out each dough ball into a 6-inch
round, placing them, without overlapping, on baking sheets as you go.
With your fingers, spread a thin layer of the topping you are using over
the surface, all the way to the edges of each pizza.

One sheet at a time, bake the pizzas on the bottom rack of the oven
until beginning to turn golden around the edges, about 6 minutes. Transfer the baking sheet to the top of the oven and bake until the crusts are
lightly brown on the bottom, 6 to 8 minutes. Garnish as indicated in the
topping recipe you are using. Serve right away.

FAMILY VARIATIONS ON THE THEME
OF ARMENIAN PIZZA

Once, in a moment of party enthusiasm, I offered to turn out cocktail tidbit–size Armenian pizzas as part of the menu for the elegant, black-tie opening of the new art gallery at the California College of Arts and Crafts. My son, Jenan, then about six years old, was conscripted to help,

My son, Jenan Wise, 2003, age 18.

and he did, popping one freshly cooked, precious, dollar-size lahmajoun into his mouth for every three he was supposed to be topping. The next day, not having had his fill, he was insistent that only Armenian pizzas would do for lunch. I agreed to turn out a batch, but I made them quite a bit larger—less rolling, less work altogether. In one of the surprising end runs a parent never quite expects from a child, Jenan was convinced they weren't the same as the tiny ones; the larger ones were like ordinary pizza! To his child's eye and mind, the cocktail tidbits were his size, and they tasted better. (Heaven knows what his reaction would have been at cousin Gary's Uncle Hagopian's, where the wide-diameter, folded-over interpretation of lahmajoun was taken to its limit: The crust was rolled out to dinner-plate size, then the lahmajoun was folded twice to make a thick, layered affair like a stacked sandwich.) Hoping to recoup the situation and the work I'd put into the special treat, I explained, "Lunch pizzas are always bigger; you can pick off little bites to nibble as you go." Jenan reluctantly adjusted his Armenian pizza gestalt and enjoyed the "normal"-size lahmajouns. I suggest you, too, adjust the size of your lahmajouns to suit the needs and time constraints of the occasion.

TRADITIONAL LAMB TOPPING FOR
ARMENIAN PIZZAS

The traditional lamb topping for lahmajoun is a prized treat from a world where meat was rare. Rich and savory as it is, a little goes a long way to satisfy. Practically speaking, if you use too much, you'll weigh down the dough to the point of sogginess, so a light hand is necessary for the right balance between crust and topping.

For ten to sixteen 6-inch pizzas

½ pound lean ground lamb

1 green bell pepper, seeded and finely chopped
(about 1 cup)

1 yellow or white onion, finely chopped (about 1 cup)

½ cup chopped fresh flat-leaf parsley

1 teaspoon chopped fresh oregano or ½ teaspoon dried

3 tablespoons tomato paste

¼ teaspoon Aleppo pepper or mild paprika

¼ teaspoon freshly ground black pepper

1½ teaspoons kosher salt

Melted butter or lemon wedges, for serving

Place all the ingredients, except the butter or lemon wedges, in a large bowl and mix thoroughly. Spread about 2 tablespoons on each rolled-out lahmajoun, covering them all the way to the edges. Bake as directed on page 71.

Garnish with a little melted butter or a squeeze of lemon juice and serve.

❖

TWO MODERN TOPPINGS FOR ARMENIAN PIZZAS

I learned to make Armenian pizzas at my mother's knee. I never depart from her dough recipe—its flavor and texture are perfect—but that doesn't stop me from dreaming up my own innovations for the topping. Following are two of my favorites. In each one, an allium (leek or onion) replaces the lamb. After all, onions—stalk or globe, cooked or raw—and pizza go together, and either variation provides delicious, meatless pizzas.

The author at age 3½.

Note: With these toppings, serve the lahmajouns soon after baking. The leeks or onions make the crust soggy if the pizzas are left too long, and the cheese becomes less than tender when cool and downright rubbery if refrigerated and reheated.

Wilted Leek and Fontina Cheese Topping

2 tablespoons extra virgin olive oil

4 leeks, thinly sliced, well washed, and drained

1 teaspoon chopped fresh thyme

½ teaspoon kosher salt

¼ cup water

8 ounces fontina cheese, coarsely grated

3 lemons, cut into 10 to 16 wedges, for garnish

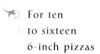 For ten to sixteen 6-inch pizzas

Heat the oil in a large sauté pan over medium-high heat. Add the leeks, thyme, salt, and water and bring to a boil. Decrease the heat to medium and cook until the leeks are soft, about 8 minutes. Drain in a colander, then pat dry. Spread on rolled-out lahmajouns and sprinkle the cheese over the top. Bake as directed on page 71. Garnish with a lemon wedge and serve right away.

Onion Confit and Pecan Topping

2 tablespoons butter

2 tablespoons extra virgin olive oil

2 large yellow onions, halved lengthwise and thinly sliced

½ teaspoon kosher salt

¼ teaspoon freshly ground black pepper

1 cup pecan halves, toasted

Parmesan cheese, shaved or finely grated, for garnish

For ten to sixteen 6-inch pizzas

Heat the butter and oil in a large sauté pan over medium-high heat until the butter melts. Add the onions, salt, and pepper and cook, stirring occasionally, until soft and beginning to turn golden, about 20 minutes. Spread on rolled-out lahmajouns and sprinkle the pecans over the top. Bake as directed on page 71. Garnish with the cheese and serve right away.

Aintab-Style Lahmajoun with Fried Eggplant, Tomato, and Green Bell Pepper

This version of lahmajoun is popular in Aintab (now called Gazientep) in Turkey, where many of my father's family came from, though his immediate family was from Marash.

Makes 10 pizzas

1 recipe lahmajoun dough (page 70)
20 slices Fried Eggplant (page 216)
20 thin, large tomato slices
20 thin green bell pepper slices, seeded
1 tablespoon chopped fresh oregano leaves or 1½
    teaspoons dried oregano
Extra virgin olive oil, for drizzling over the lahmajoun
Kosher salt

Preheat the oven to 475°F.

Divide the lahmajoun dough into 10 parts. Roll each out into an 8- to 10-inch round and place the rounds on baking sheets without touching, as described on page 71.

Arrange 2 eggplant slices, 2 tomato slices, and 2 bell pepper slices over each round. Sprinkle with oregano, drizzle with olive oil, and season with salt. Bake as described on page 71, until the bottoms are golden and the tomato and pepper slices are soft. Serve right away or at room temperature, either open face or folded in half.

Basic Boerek Triangles

The savory pastries known as boereks (also beureks, buereks, boeregs, or beoregs) are always part of the Armenian maza table. They take many shapes, from triangles to rolls, crescents, and whole rectangular pies. Except for El-Boerek (page 83), made with a pielike dough, and Sou-Boerek (page 85), made with egg noodle pasta dough, they are usually made with fillo dough. My grandmother made her own fillo, but that was before the days of excellent commercial products available in boxes in the freezer section of most supermarkets. For swift and effortless boerek making, I recommend you go with the modern flow, and buy ready-made fillo. The only trick to working with fillo is to keep it covered with a damp cloth until ready to butter, fill, and fold each boerek so that the stack of sheets doesn't dry out.

Following are general instructions for preparing fillo triangles (easier and neater than rolls). While many cooks like to butter each fillo sheet, I prefer stacking them in twos, then buttering the top layer only. This results in crisper, less caloric boereks.

For each triangle, you will need:

> 1 (8 × 13-inch) sheet fillo
> Melted butter, for brushing on the fillo
> 1 heaping tablespoon filling (recipes follow, pages 78–80)

Cut the fillo sheet lengthwise in half to make two strips approximately 4 inches wide by 13 inches long. Lay one strip on top of another and brush the top strip with butter. Place about 1 tablespoon of the filling mixture in a bottom corner and fold over the dough to make a triangle and enclose the filling. Continue folding up, flag style, to the top of the strip. Brush the seam with butter to seal it and place the boerek seam-side down on a baking sheet. Brush the top with butter. Continue with as many triangles as you are making, arranging them on the baking sheet without touching. (You will probably need more than one baking sheet.) Bake at 375°F until golden and crispy, about 15 minutes.

Boereks may be prepared in advance: without brushing the tops with butter, wrap them in plastic wrap and refrigerate overnight or freeze for up to 2 weeks (defrost before baking). When ready to serve, brush the tops with butter and bake as above.

TRADITIONAL CHEESE BOEREK FILLING TWO WAYS

Makes 24 triangles

2 large eggs
¾ pound Monterey jack or Muenster cheese, shredded,
    or a mixture of 6 ounces cottage cheese and
    6 ounces crumbled feta
½ cup chopped fresh flat-leaf parsley
24 (8 × 13-inch) sheets fillo
8 tablespoons melted butter, for brushing the fillo

Preheat the oven to 375°F.

Break the eggs into a bowl and whisk until frothy. Stir in the cheese and parsley. Use the mixture to fill and fold 24 fillo triangles as described on pages 77–78.

Arrange on baking sheets without touching and bake until golden and crispy, about 15 minutes. Serve right away or at room temperature.

CHEESE AND STEWED GRAPE LEAF FILLING FOR BOEREK

4 ounces Homemade Fresh Cheese (page 48) or feta,
   crumbled
1 cup Grape Leaves Stewed with Tomato and Lemon
   (page 222), drained and chopped
20 (8 × 13-inch) sheets fillo
6 tablespoons melted butter, for brushing the fillo

Makes 20
triangles

Preheat the oven to 375°F.

Place the cheese and grape leaves in a bowl and mix with a fork. Use
the mixture to fill and fold 20 fillo triangles as described on pages 77–78.

Arrange on baking sheets without touching and bake until golden and
crispy, about 15 minutes. Serve right away or at room temperature.

GOAT CHEESE, GARLIC, AND HERB FILLING FOR BOEREK

4 ounces soft goat cheese, at room temperature
1 small clove garlic, minced or pressed
1 tablespoon chopped fresh chives
½ teaspoon chopped fresh oregano
¼ cup chopped fresh flat-leaf parsley
2 teaspoons extra virgin olive oil
12 (8 × 13-inch) sheets fillo
4 tablespoons (½ stick) melted butter, for brushing the fillo

Makes 12
triangles

Preheat the oven to 375°F.

Combine the cheese, garlic, chives, oregano, parsley, and olive oil in a
bowl and stir with a fork to mix well. Use the mixture to fill and fold 12
fillo triangles as described on pages 77–78.

Arrange on baking sheets without touching and bake until golden and
crispy, about 15 minutes. Serve right away or at room temperature.

BUTTERNUT SQUASH FILLING FOR BOEREK

Makes 16 triangles

½ pound butternut squash, peeled, seeded,
    and coarsely grated (about 2 cups)
½ cup cooked long grain white rice (page 231)
2 scallions, white and light green part, finely chopped
1 tablespoon chopped cilantro
3 tablespoons crumbled feta or Homemade
    Fresh Cheese (page 48)
Kosher salt
16 (8 × 13-inch) sheets fillo
6 tablespoons melted butter, for brushing the fillo

Preheat the oven to 375°F.

In a bowl, mix together the squash, rice, scallions, cilantro, cheese, and salt to taste. Use the mixture to fill and fold 16 fillo triangles, as described on pages 77–78.

Arrange on baking sheets without touching and bake until golden and crispy, about 15 minutes. Serve right away or at room temperature.

BUTTERNUT SQUASH BOEREK AS PIE

You can make this boerek in pie form, as described for Spinach Fillo Pie (page 81). It makes a lovely, light meal entrée, especially if you include ¼ cup toasted pine nuts in the filling. Bake at 375°F for 45 minutes.

Spinach Fillo Pie

Fillo pies are a popular entrée, especially in the Eastern Mediterranean strain of Armenian cooking. In pie form, fillo boerek is very easy to make because you can layer the ingredients in one large dish without having to roll up individual pieces.

Makes one 9 × 11-inch pie; serves 6 to 8 as an entrée

1½ pounds (about 2 bunches) spinach, stems removed, leaves coarsely chopped, well washed, and drained

2 tablespoons extra virgin olive oil, plus extra for greasing the baking dish

1 medium yellow or white onion, finely chopped

¼ cup chopped fresh flat-leaf parsley leaves

8 ounces feta cheese, crumbled

3 large eggs, lightly beaten

Kosher salt

12 (8 × 13-inch) sheets fillo

6 tablespoons melted butter, for brushing on the fillo

Preheat the oven to 375°F. Lightly grease a 9 × 12-inch-deep baking dish.

Place the still-moist spinach in a large nonreactive pot or skillet and stir over medium heat for 3 to 4 minutes, until wilted but still bright green. Drain in a colander and set aside to cool. Before using, squeeze out excess moisture without wringing the spinach dry.

Heat the oil in a medium sauté pan over medium-high heat. Stir in the onion and cook until beginning to wilt, 3 to 4 minutes. Stir in the spinach, parsley, cheese, and eggs, and season with salt to taste. Set aside without further cooking.

To assemble the pie, place 2 sheets of fillo in the dish and brush the top sheet with butter. Continue layering with 2 more sheets, brush with butter, and then another 2 sheets, top sheet brushed with butter. Spread the spinach mixture over the layers. Top with the remaining sheets of fillo, brushing every other sheet with butter as you go, as before. Finally, brush the top with butter.

Bake until golden and crisp, about 45 minutes. Serve right away or at room temperature.

Spinach pie may be cooled, covered, and stored in the refrigerator for up to 2 days. Remove from the refrigerator 30 minutes before serving and serve at room temperature, or reheat in a 350°F oven.

Spinach Tahini Boerek
El-Boerek

This boerek calls for a different dough and a tahini-flavored filling. The pastry is formed into small crescent-shaped turnovers, like empanadas. The simple dough can also be filled with a cheese filling (pages 78–79) or with any of the other fillings in this chapter.

 Makes eighteen 4-inch crescents

Dough

1½ cups all-purpose flour, plus extra for rolling out the dough
½ teaspoon kosher salt
½ cup (1 stick) butter, cut into ½-inch bits
3 tablespoons cold water

Filling

4 tablespoons butter
1 medium yellow or white onion, finely chopped
2 scallions, white and light green part, finely chopped
½ pound trimmed spinach leaves (from a ¾-pound bunch),
    chopped, washed, and drained (6 packed cups)

½ teaspoon kosher salt

¼ cup tahini

½ cup medium-fine fresh breadcrumbs

¼ teaspoon freshly ground black pepper

Butter for greasing the baking sheets

1 egg, lightly beaten, for glazing the boereks

To make the dough, place the flour and salt in a food processor and pulse 3 times to mix. Add the butter and pulse until evenly crumbly. Add the water and process just until you can gather up the dough. Wrap the dough in plastic wrap and press into a smooth disk. Set aside to rest in the refrigerator for 1 hour, or up to 2 days. Remove 20 minutes before using.

To make the filling, melt the butter in a large sauté pan over medium-high heat. Add the onion and scallion and cook until wilted, 3 minutes. Stir in the spinach and salt and continue cooking until the spinach is well wilted and most of the liquid is gone, about 4 minutes. Add the tahini, breadcrumbs, and pepper and stir to mix. Remove from the heat and set aside to cool.

Preheat the oven to 350°F. Lightly grease 2 baking sheets with butter.

On a lightly floured surface, roll out the dough into an 18-inch circle, lightly reflouring the surface and top of the dough as you go to keep it from sticking. Cut into 4-inch circles (a 28-ounce can of tomatoes is a good cutter). Place 1 tablespoon of the filling in the center of each circle. Fold over to make a half-moon shape. Pinch together the edges to seal and place on the baking sheets. Gather up the dough scraps and roll out again, as thinly as possible. Fill, fold, and seal as above.

Brush the tops of the boereks with the egg glaze and bake for 20 minutes, until golden and cooked through. Serve warm or at room temperature.

An Ancient Noodle Dish
Sou-Boerek

Sou-boerek is sometimes described as water pastry because the dough, like an egg pasta dough, is rolled thin and parboiled before assembling the dish. I prefer to describe it as Armenian lasagne cum mac-and-cheese. I offer the recipe here for those who enjoy the old art of pasta-making, working the triceps as the dough is rolled out, and contemplating ancient ways in the kitchen while doing so. I also offer a modern tip: Since Sou-boerek is basically a pasta (fresh lasagne sheets from a pasta store can substitute), you can knead more flour into the dough to make it stiff enough to pass through a pasta machine, then let the machine do the hefty work of rolling out the dough. Don't worry if the individual layers from hand-rolling turn out a little raggedy and fragile. Just keep adding flour as you roll them out to make them as manageable as possible; once blanched in the water, the sheets become firm and easy to handle.

Serves 12 as a maza, 6 as an entrée

Dough

3 large eggs

½ teaspoon kosher salt

1 tablespoon extra virgin olive oil

1½ cups all-purpose flour, plus up to 2 cups more for kneading and rolling out the dough

Recipe continues on next page

Filling

> 5 tablespoons butter, melted, for brushing the layers
> 3/4 pound good melting cheese, such as Monterey jack, Muenster, Greek kefalotyri, or mild white cheddar, coarsely grated
> 1/2 cup chopped fresh flat-leaf parsley

To make the dough, crack the eggs into a large bowl and beat with an electric mixer. Beat in the salt and olive oil. Beat in the 1½ cups flour to make a sticky dough. By hand, knead in more flour, up to ½ cup, to make a dough you can gather into a ball. Transfer the dough ball to a counter and continue kneading in more flour, up to ¾ cup, until you have a smooth, cohesive, somewhat soft dough.

Divide the dough into 6 equal portions, pat each into a ball, and set the balls on a counter or baking sheet without touching each other. Cover with a kitchen towel and let rest for 1 hour, or up to several hours.

To roll out and precook the dough sheets, bring a large pot of salted water to boil. Have ready a large bowl of cold water. On a floured surface, roll out each dough ball into a thin 10-inch round. Flour the counter and the top of the dough as you go to get as few holes in each round as possible. As you roll them out, drop the sheets into the boiling water and cook for 30 seconds, pressing the sheet into the water so it cooks through. With tongs, lift the cooked sheet out of the water and transfer it to the cold-water bath. Lift the sheets out of the cold-water bath, shake them dry a little, and spread them out on paper towels to dry. Continue this process until all 6 dough sheets are precooked and laid out to dry. They may rest this way for up to several hours.

To assemble the sou-boerek, preheat the oven to 400°F. Lightly butter a 9 to 10-inch square or rectangular baking dish with some of the melted butter.

Layer 3 precooked sheets on the bottom of the dish, lightly brushing each layer with butter. Spread the shredded cheese over the third layer and sprinkle the parsley over the cheese. Top with the remaining 3 sheets, lightly buttering each as you go. Place in the oven and bake for 30 to 35 minutes, until golden and crispy across the top. Let sit for 5 minutes, then cut into portions and serve warm or at room temperature.

The sou-boerek may also be reheated briefly in an oven. Cooled and wrapped in plastic wrap, it will keep in the refrigerator for 2 days. Bring it to room temperature before reheating.

Salads:
Old World and New

❖

A salad of fresh and/or cooked ingredients is a customary part of an Armenian meal, usually served alongside the entrée. In this chapter, I give free rein to imagination with seven composed salads in the Armenian spirit, but with California style. In a further nod to California style, I often serve them as a separate course.

Armenian Chopped Tomato Salad with Green Bell Pepper, Cucumber, and Iceberg Lettuce

Serves 4

When I was growing up, we always had this and rice pilaf as accompaniments to simple meat entrées such as grilled lamb chops. Iceberg lettuce is essential. Nothing compares to its watery crunch for bringing together the other elements in a way that moistens the pilaf without requiring any oil.

2 large ripe tomatoes, coarsely chopped into ½-inch chunks

1 green bell pepper, coarsely chopped into ¼-inch chunks

1 large pickling cucumber or small regular cucumber, partially peeled in stripes, and coarsely chopped into ½-inch chunks

½ head iceberg lettuce, cut into ¼-inch-wide strips

2 scallions, white and light green part, trimmed and finely chopped

¼ cup chopped fresh flat-leaf parsley

2 tablespoons freshly squeezed lemon juice

Kosher salt and freshly ground black pepper, to taste

Combine all the ingredients in a medium bowl and toss to mix. Serve right away or set aside at room temperature for up to 20 minutes.

Layered Tomato Salad with Green Bell Pepper, Wilted Onion, and Parsley

This is a salad for the height of the fresh tomato season, late summer to early fall, when tomatoes deserve being featured on a platter. It's a perfect red, tart addition to a summer menu.

Serves 4

½ yellow, white, or red onion, thinly sliced
¼ teaspoon kosher salt
2 large ripe tomatoes, sliced ½ inch thick
½ green bell pepper, thinly slivered lengthwise
¼ cup chopped fresh flat-leaf parsley
1½ tablespoons red wine vinegar
3 tablespoons extra virgin olive oil
Extra kosher salt and freshly ground black pepper,
    to taste

In a small bowl, toss together the onion slices and ¼ teaspoon salt. Set aside for 15 to 30 minutes while preparing the remaining ingredients.

To assemble the salad, arrange the tomato slices on a serving platter. Strew the bell pepper, onion, and parsley over the tomatoes. Sprinkle with the vinegar, then with the oil and extra salt and pepper to taste. Serve without tossing.

Salads: Old World and New · 91

Black-Eyed Pea Salad with Black Olives and Tomatoes

Chickpeas, cranberry beans, red kidney beans, or lima beans can substitute for the black-eyed peas in this legumy salad. Though recipes often call for already-cooked canned peas or beans, I find all the products I've tasted too soft and salty. Instead, I recommend pressure cooking; it's a fast and easy way to prepare earthy-tasting, plump legumes that aren't mushy.

Serves 4 to 6

1 cup dried black-eyed peas

4 cups water

½ teaspoon kosher salt

1 large tomato, peeled, seeded, and cut lengthwise into
  ½-inch-wide strips

⅓ cup Kalamata olives, pitted if desired

¼ cup finely chopped yellow or white onion

¼ cup chopped fresh flat-leaf parsley

1 tablespoon red wine vinegar

1 tablespoon freshly squeezed lemon juice

½ teaspoon Aleppo pepper

Kosher salt, to taste

2 tablespoons extra virgin olive oil

Place the black-eyed peas and water in a pressure cooker or large pot.

To pressure-cook: Lock on the lid and bring to pressure over high heat, about 5 minutes. Decrease the heat to medium-high and cook for 5 minutes. Remove from the heat and set aside for 5 minutes. Gently release any remaining pressure and remove the lid.

To cook on the stove top: Bring to a boil over high heat. Decrease the heat to maintain a brisk simmer and cook for 25 minutes, until the peas are tender but not collapsing. Remove from the heat and let sit for 5 minutes to cool and settle down.

Either way, stir in the ½ teaspoon salt and set aside to cool for 5 minutes more.

To assemble the salad, drain the peas. In a large bowl, combine them with the remaining ingredients and toss to mix. Serve right away, or chill first. Will keep in the refrigerator for up to 2 days.

AGE-OLD LEGUME WISDOM

Salt is added at the end of the cooking process for a good reason: so that it can easily penetrate and season the legumes. If added at the beginning, it toughens the skin, and the result is tough beans.

If cooking the black-eyed peas (or any other dried legume) in advance, let them cool in the cooking liquid all the way to room temperature, then refrigerate them in the liquid. They will keep this way for up to 5 days.

Fresh Fava Bean Salad with String Cheese and Chive Oil

Fava beans, cooked fresh in spring and early summer, sparkle in a salad embellished with another Old World gem, Armenian string cheese.

5 pounds fava beans, in their pods
2 teaspoons chopped fresh mint leaves
1 tablespoon extra virgin olive oil
1½ teaspoons freshly ground black pepper
4 large butter lettuce leaves
1 cup String Cheese shreds (page 46)

Chive Oil

¼ packed cup chopped fresh chives
¼ cup extra virgin olive oil
¼ teaspoon kosher salt

Shell the fava beans and blanch them for 5 minutes in boiling water. Drain, cool under cold water, and peel. Set aside.

To make the chive oil, bring a small pot of water to boil. Add the chives and right away drain them in a colander. Transfer them to paper towels and pat dry. In a food processor or blender, puree the chives with the oil and salt. Set aside.

To make the salad, toss together the favas, mint, olive oil, and pepper.

Place the lettuce leaves on a platter or individual plates. Mound the favas on the lettuce and scatter the string cheese across the top. Drizzle with the chive oil and serve.

FAVA BEAN FERVOR

My enthusiasm for fresh fava beans is unbounded, to the extent that I plant many each year so that I can reap their benefits for both the garden and the table. I look forward to their large, pealike flowers with black centers that grace the early spring garden in a decorative way. A little later, in late spring and on to summer, their beans provide legumy goodness to salads and stews. All the while, they are doing garden service as a nitrogen-fixing plant. Later still, when the pods are large, almost bursting at the seam, and the beans have become bitter and my thumbs don't want to shell another fava (they are a very prolific plant!), they fulfill their destiny by being added to the compost pile to decompose and make rich and nutritious fertilizer for next year's garden.

Lentil Salad with Walnut Oil and Yogurt Cheese Balls

Serves 6

A salad similar to this was one of the most popular dishes at my Pig-by-the-Tail delicatessen. Indeed, there were some customers who came in for a pint of it for their lunch on a daily basis. In those days, I made it with feta cheese; for this book, I have revised the recipe to call for yogurt cheese balls. They're an equally yummy cheese pairing for the lentils, and, if you don't have the yogurt cheese balls, I suggest using a good quality Bulgarian, Greek, or Israeli feta cheese. French green lentils, for their nutty flavor and firm texture when cooked, are my choice for the salad.

1½ cups French green lentils

5 scallions, white and light green part, ever-so-
    thinly sliced into rounds

¼ cup chopped fresh flat-leaf parsley

⅓ cup freshly squeezed lemon juice

½ cup walnut oil

Kosher salt and freshly ground black pepper, to taste

2 tablespoons chopped fresh scallion tops, for garnish

6 yogurt cheese balls (page 50) or 4 ounces feta cheese,
    crumbled

Place the lentils in a large pot, add water to cover by 1½ inches, and bring to a boil over high heat. Decrease the heat to medium-high and cook until al dente, about 17 minutes. Drain in a colander, cool under cold running water from the tap, and set aside to drip dry for 20 minutes or so.

To assemble the salad, place the lentils in a large serving bowl. Add the sliced scallions, parsley, lemon juice, and walnut oil. Toss to mix and season with salt and pepper to taste. Just before serving, garnish with the cheese and chopped scallion tops.

Wilted Baby Spinach Salad with Toasted Walnuts and Pomegranate Vinaigrette

Serves 4

My Uncle Bob, my father's eldest brother, and his wife, Aunt Queenie, were my godparents. Outside the kitchen door of their Sacramento house was a glorious pomegranate tree, and it was there that I learned to love pomegranates. This salad is inspired by that tree, and the fun days we had sitting in their kitchen on autumn days, munching on Queenie's tourshi and cracker bread before dinner as we opened freshly picked pomegranates. No one seemed to mind the red juice that spilled out of the fruit and stained our hands—there were plenty of napkins.

8 cups baby spinach leaves

3 tablespoons extra virgin olive oil

1 cup walnut pieces

3 tablespoons pomegranate syrup

1½ tablespoons red wine vinegar

Kosher salt, to taste

½ cup pomegranate seeds (optional, see box, page 99)

Place the spinach in a large salad bowl and set aside.

Heat 1½ tablespoons of the oil in a large sauté pan over medium heat. Add the walnuts and cook, stirring frequently, until toasted, 3 to 4 minutes. Increase the heat to medium-high, add the pomegranate molasses and vinegar, and stir to mix. While hot, add this dressing to the spinach, along with the remaining oil, and season with salt. Sprinkle the pomegranate seeds, if using, over the top and serve right away, while still warm.

GETTING TO THE SEEDS OF POMEGRANATES

The least messy way to get the seeds out of a pomegranate is first to cut the fruit into quarters lengthwise. Then, put the quarters into a large bowl of cold water and pull off the outside "skin." Discard the skin and, with your fingers, separate the seeds from their enclosing membrane sacs. The seeds will fall into the water and the membrane pieces will rise to the top. Lift off the membrane pieces and discard them. Drain the seeds in a colander. Use them whole to garnish salads or wherever else you'd like a ruby red, tart, crunchy spark to the dish.

Tabbouli

The trick to making a truly fine tabbouli is to let the bulgur rehydrate in plenty of water for a good hour (but not longer or it becomes starchy), and then to let it drain for half an hour, so the tabbouli is fluffy, not soggy.

Makes 8 cups

1½ cups medium bulgur
Water
1 cucumber, peeled, seeded, and finely chopped
1 green bell pepper, finely chopped
2 tomatoes, finely chopped
2 scallions, light green part only, finely chopped
¼ cup chopped fresh mint leaves
½ cup chopped fresh flat-leaf parsley leaves
½ cup freshly squeezed lemon juice
1½ teaspoons kosher salt, or to taste

Place the bulgur in a large bowl and add water to the top. Gently pour off the water and repeat twice until the water looks clear. Add water again, enough to cover the grains by 2 inches, and set aside to soak for 1 hour.

Drain the bulgur in a colander and set aside to drip dry for 30 minutes. Transfer to a large bowl and add the remaining ingredients. Toss to mix and distribute the vegetables evenly. Serve right away, or set aside at room temperature for up to 3 hours, or refrigerate for up to 3 days.

New World Melon Salad
with Mock Basterma

⌐ Serves 4 to 6

When I was growing up, melon played a prominent role on our summer table: watermelon, cantaloupe, and, especially prized, honeydews were chilled, sliced, and served without further ado, except for a sprinkle of salt just before eating. In this rather fancy rendition of that treat, mock basterma stands in for the salt element and there's a bit of lemon and oil to gild the lily. Taking the dish back to its Italian home, prosciutto can substitute for the basterma.

> 3 cups watercress, leaves and tender stems only
> ½ honeydew melon
> 2 teaspoons freshly squeezed lemon juice
> 12 slices Mock Basterma (page 43)
> ½ teaspoon freshly ground black pepper
> 2 tablespoons walnut or hazelnut oil

Spread the watercress on a large platter. Scoop the seeds out of the melon, cut it into thin, half-moon slices, and cut off the rind. Arrange the melon slices over the watercress. Sprinkle the lemon juice over the melon and cress. Drape the basterma slices over the melon and sprinkle the pepper over the basterma. Drizzle the oil over all and serve.

"Meat"balls: Kufta

❖

Kufta. Keufteh. Kibbe. Filled or not; with meat and bulgur, bulgur alone, or a legume (chickpeas, lentils); served raw, poached, fried, or baked, and hot or cold, these versatile "meat"balls are a staple of Caucasian, Middle Eastern, Eastern Mediterranean, and Jewish cooking from Armenia to Turkey, Greece, Lebanon, Syria, Israel, Iran, Iraq, Afghanistan, North Africa, and all the other places where people of those lands and cultures have settled today. They're a delight of home meals and a treat on banquet tables. In this chapter, I include a panoply of them, with easy instructions and some tips on how to turn out perfect kufta, even if you're a novice at this fine home art.

Armenian Steak Tartar, with Garnishes
Chee Kufta

I can still hear my father's voice as he explained to us kids while my mother kneaded the mixture for chee kufta, that, for this Armenian tartar, a raw meat delicacy, the bulgur has to be fine, not medium, and the lamb must be of extra-special quality. He had trimmed, boned, and degristled every morsel of meat from a leg of lamb, separating out the parts to cube for shish kebab, those for grinding for kufta, and the trim, never to be made light of, for simmering into Fasulya, the famous green bean, tomato, and lamb soup/stew (page 141). We had an old-fashioned, manual countertop meat grinder kept especially for this. A dish to showcase the excellence of the meat, chee kufta always got the best part and Dad did the grinding himself, twice. Armenians often include some minced green bell pepper in the mix and a little more as garnish, but Dad didn't, and I don't.

Makes 18 to 20 kuftas, serves 6

¾ cup fine bulgur

½ cup water

½ pound high-quality, lean, finely ground lamb

½ small yellow or white onion, minced (½ cup)

1 scallion, white and light green part, minced

2 tablespoons finely chopped flat-leaf parsley

¼ teaspoon Aleppo pepper

1 teaspoon kosher salt

Garnishes

> 2 tablespoons finely chopped fresh flat-leaf parsley
>
> 1 scallion, white and light green part, minced
>
> 2 tablespoons finely chopped green bell pepper
>   (optional)
>
> 2 tomatoes, cut into 8 wedges each

Place the bulgur and water in a bowl and set aside to soak for 15 minutes.

Add the lamb, onion, scallion, parsley, Aleppo pepper, and salt. With your hands, knead the mixture until well blended and smooth, 2 to 3 minutes, adding a little more water if necessary to keep it from drying out. Pat the mixture into 1-inch balls and arrange them on a serving platter. Sprinkle the chopped garnishes over the top and set the tomato wedges around and about. Serve right away.

KUFTA-MAKING AND COOKING TIPS

❖ The kufta mixture requires kneading to bring the ingredients together and break down the meat fibers. Doing this by hand takes some elbow grease and about 15 minutes. For ease, I use a food processor, pulsing quickly just until the mixture coheres.

❖ The kufta mixture should be chilled before forming into balls. This allows the dry ingredients to soak up the moisture and become firm so you can make balls that won't flatten and sink into themselves before they're even in the pot.

❖ When patting the kufta into balls, use a light touch and moist hands.

❖ When poaching kufta, adjust the heat from time to time to keep the liquid at a noticeable simmer, but not a hard boil.

Basic Kufta Mixture
Keyma

Basic kufta can be made with lamb or beef, and filled or not.

Makes enough for 1 recipe of Tray Kufta or 18 to 20 stuffed kufta

¾ cup medium or fine bulgur

½ cup water

½ pound finely ground lean lamb

1 small yellow or white onion, minced

¼ teaspoon ground allspice

Pinch of cinnamon (optional)

¼ teaspoon Aleppo pepper

1 teaspoon kosher salt

Combine the bulgur and water in a large bowl and set aside to soak for 15 minutes.

Add the remaining ingredients and knead with an electric mixer or in a food processor until the mixture is smooth and pasty, about 5 minutes with the mixer, 3 minutes in the processor. Set aside in the refrigerator to chill and firm for 1 hour, or up to several hours. Proceed with the filling recipe you are using.

Tray Kufta
Sini Kufta

A homey version of stuffed kufta, sini kufta is very easy to assemble and bake without having to form precise, smooth balls. It is usually served with a vegetable side or tossed salad. Sini kufta may be prepared and frozen in its tray for up to 2 weeks before cooking.

Butter, for greasing the baking dish
1 recipe Basic Kufta Mixture (page 106)
1 recipe Basic Meat and Nut Filling (page 108),
    made with lamb or beef and walnuts
2 tablespoons melted butter, for baking the kufta
¼ cup water

Preheat the oven to 400°F. Lightly grease a 2- to 3-quart square or rectangular baking dish with butter.

Spread half of the kufta mixture on the bottom of the baking dish, patting it down lightly with wet hands to make an even, unbroken layer. Spread the filling over the top. Dollop the remaining kufta mixture over the filling and, with wet hands, spread it out to cover the entire top. Score through the top layer to divide into diamond- or square-shaped sections. Pour the melted butter over the surface and sprinkle with the water. Bake until cooked through and no longer soft, about 25 minutes. Remove and cool for 5 to 10 minutes.

Cut into portions according to the scored shapes and serve hot or at room temperature.

Basic Meat and Nut Filling for Kufta

Made with lamb or beef and walnuts, this filling is used for Tray Kufta (page 107); made with lamb and walnuts or pine nuts, it fills Harput Kufta (page 109).

Fills 1 recipe of Tray Kufta or 35 kufta balls

> 3 tablespoons butter
> 1 large yellow or white onion, minced
> $\frac{1}{2}$ pound finely ground lamb or beef
> $\frac{1}{2}$ cup walnut pieces or pine nuts, minced but not
>   pulverized
> $\frac{1}{4}$ teaspoon ground allspice
> 1 teaspoon kosher salt
> $\frac{1}{2}$ teaspoon freshly ground black pepper

Melt the butter in a large sauté pan over medium-high heat. Add the onion and cook, stirring occasionally, for 5 minutes, until no longer raw. Add the meat, decrease the heat to medium, and continue cooking, stirring to break up the chunks, until the meat is no longer pink, 3 to 4 minutes. Mix in the nuts, allspice, salt, and pepper. Remove from the heat, cool slightly, and refrigerate to chill for 1 hour, or up to 3 days. Knead briefly before using.

Kufta with Lamb and Walnut
or Pine Nut Stuffing
Harput Kufta

Learning to fill and form light and airy stuffed kufta balls is part of growing up female in an Armenian home, and happy hours are spent with one's mother and sometimes assorted female relatives tutoring young hands in the craft. Harput kuftas are a deluxe dish of Armenian cooking and a speciality of the town of Harput, where the kuftas are given extra flavor by poaching them in meat stock seasoned with tomato rather than just water. Harput kuftas are not difficult to make; I suspect the lessons are as much for cheerful, multigenerational playing together in the kitchen as they are for serious instruction.

Makes 18 to
20 kuftas,
serves 4 to 6

1 recipe Basic Meat and Nut Filling (page 108), made
    with lamb and walnuts or pine nuts, chilled
1 recipe Basic Kufta Mixture (page 106), made with lamb,
    chilled
8 cups low-sodium chicken broth
2 tablespoons tomato paste
1½ teaspoons kosher salt
1 cup yogurt, stirred smooth, for serving
New Wave Vegetable Garnish (optional, see box, page 110)

Make the filling first so it can be cooked and begin to chill while making the shell mixture.

Form the kufta mixture into 1½- to 2-inch smooth balls. With moist hands, hold a ball in one hand and make an indentation in the ball with the thumb of your other hand. Rotate the ball as you gently hollow it out until it is as thin as possible without tearing. Place 1 tablespoon of the filling in the hollow and, still with moist hands, reshape the kufta into a smooth ball. Continue until all the kuftas are filled. Cook right away, or wrap and freeze for up to 3 weeks. (Frozen kuftas may be cooked without defrosting; they will take a little longer.)

To cook the kuftas, combine the broth, tomato paste, and salt in a large pot and bring to a boil over high heat. Add the kuftas and bring back to a boil. Decrease the heat to maintain a simmer, and cook, uncovered, until the kuftas rise to the surface, about 5 minutes.

With a wire strainer, ladle the kuftas into individual bowls, moisten with some of the broth, and garnish with the vegetable mixture, if using. Serve hot, with the yogurt on the side.

NEW WAVE VEGETABLE GARNISH
FOR HARPUT KUFTA

I like to embellish Harput kuftas with this fresh vegetable garnish for color and crunch.

    4 ounces baby green beans
    1 large tomato, seeded and coarsely chopped
    1 cup finely shredded green cabbage
    2 tablespoons extra virgin olive oil
    Kosher salt and freshly ground black pepper,
        to taste

Cook the green beans in boiling water until limp but still bright green, about 5 minutes. Drain, pat dry on paper towels, and place in a bowl. Add the remaining ingredients and toss to mix. Use right away, or set aside at room temperature for up to 3 hours.

Izmir or Smyrna Kufta

Izmir (formerly called Smyrna) kuftas reflect their Turkish-Armenian origin in that Aegean city with their cumin and garlic seasoning, breadcrumbs instead of bulgur, and the addition of an egg (which I like to replace with white wine) for the moistener. They are formed into tapered ovals, sautéed or baked, and served hot or cold for an appetizer. Or sometimes they are bathed in a quick tomato sauce and served over rice pilaf or spaghetti (see page 113).

Makes 20 kuftas, serves 4 as an entrée or 6 to 8 as an appetizer

¾ pound ground lamb
1 clove garlic, minced
⅓ cup coarse fresh breadcrumbs
¼ cup chopped fresh flat-leaf parsley
⅛ teaspoon ground allspice
1 teaspoon ground cumin
1 teaspoon kosher salt
¼ teaspoon Aleppo pepper
3 tablespoons white wine or 1 small egg
2 tablespoons butter or olive oil, for sautéing

In a large bowl, combine all the ingredients except the butter and knead with your hands until well mixed. Pat into 20 teardrop-shaped, tapered ovals. Set aside in the refrigerator for 30 minutes.

To cook, heat the butter in a large heavy skillet over medium-high heat. Add the kuftas without crowding (cook in 2 batches, if necessary), and sauté, shaking the pan, until browned all around, about 5 minutes.

Decrease the heat to medium-low and cook until done but still moist, about 5 minutes. Remove from the heat and set aside in the pan for 5 minutes. Or, cool and chill in the refrigerator.

Serve hot or cold as an appetizer. Or, serve hot in tomato sauce over spaghetti or linguine (page 113).

Armenian Spaghetti and Meatballs

Often a quick tomato sauce is made with the pan juices from sautéing Izmir Kufta (page 111). Spicy Lamb or Beef Meatballs (page 114) or Butter Kufta (page 121) work as well for this Armenian version of the internationally appreciated, beloved spaghetti and meatballs.

Serves 4

1 batch Izmir Kufta (page 111)

2 medium tomatoes, peeled and seeded, or 1 cup
canned tomatoes, chopped, juices reserved

1 small green bell pepper, cut into thin slivers

1 cup low-sodium chicken broth

¾ pound spaghetti or linguine, cooked al dente and
kept warm

Sauté the kuftas as described on page 111. Transfer to a plate and set aside in a warm place.

In the same pan, combine the tomatoes, their juices, and bell pepper and cook over medium-high heat until the vegetables wilt, about 5 minutes. Add the broth and bring to a boil. Decrease the heat to medium and cook until thickened and saucy, 15 to 20 minutes.

Reheat the kuftas briefly in the sauce and serve over the pasta.

Spicy Lamb or Beef Meatballs in Tomato Cilantro Sauce

In a modern twist with ancient flavors, these Armenian-style meatballs have no bulgur or breadcrumbs; they're just meatballs pillowed in bulgur pilaf. For ease, mince the garlic, onion, and chili peppers together in a food processor.

Makes 14 walnut-size meatballs, serves 3 to 4 as an entrée or 6 to 8 as an appetizer

Meatballs

¾ pound ground lamb or beef

4 large cloves garlic, minced

½ medium yellow or white onion, minced

2 small fresh red chile peppers, such as Fresnos or cayennes, stemmed and minced

½ teaspoon ground cumin

Pinch cinnamon

⅛ teaspoon cardamon seeds, smashed

2 teaspoons finely chopped orange zest

Olive oil, for frying the meatballs

❖

Sauce

2 tablespoons butter

4 medium tomatoes, coarsely chopped, juices reserved

½ teaspoon kosher salt

¼ teaspoon Aleppo pepper

¼ cup cilantro leaves

Basic Bulgur Pilaf (page 259), warm, for serving

To make the meatballs, combine all the ingredients except the olive oil in a bowl. Mix and knead until well blended. Set aside in the refrigerator for 30 minutes, or up to overnight. Form into walnut-size meatballs and re-frigerate again until ready to use, up to overnight.

To cook the meatballs, lightly grease a heavy sauté pan with olive oil and heat over medium-high heat. Add the meatballs and cook, turning one or two times, until browned and cooked through, about 8 minutes. Transfer to a plate and set aside in a warm place.

To make the sauce, melt the butter over medium heat in the same pan as used for cooking the meatballs. Add the tomatoes, salt, and pepper, stir to mix, and sauté until the tomatoes wilt and soften. Stir in the cilantro, then add the meatballs back to the pan. Reheat briefly and serve hot over bulgur pilaf.

Kufta in Yogurt Mint Broth
Madzoon Kufta

Serves 4 to 6

In my simplified version of madzoon kufta, sometimes called Aintab kufta because it's so popular there, the kuftas are not stuffed. To make the more elaborate, ortho-dox Aintab version, fill the kuftas with Basic Meat and Nut Filling (page 108) and garnish with strips of poached chicken. Either way, for this dish the mint should be dried because it lends a subtle, less heady aroma and taste than fresh mint.

1 batch Basic Kufta Mixture (page 106)
4 cups low-sodium chicken broth
1½ teaspoons kosher salt
2 cups yogurt, drained for 30 minutes (page 24)
1 large egg
2 tablespoons butter
1 tablespoon dried mint leaves

Form the kufta into 1-inch balls. In a medium saucepan, bring the broth and salt to a boil over high heat. Add the kuftas, decrease the heat to maintain a brisk simmer, and cook for 7 to 8 minutes, until the kuftas rise up and are firm.

While the kuftas cook, whisk together the yogurt and egg in a small bowl and set aside. In a small pan, melt the butter over medium heat. Add the mint, stir to mix, and set aside in a warm place.

When the kuftas are cooked, turn off the heat. Whisk some of the poaching broth into the yogurt mixture, then pour it into the pot with the kuftas. Heat just to the boiling point, stir in the butter and mint mixture, and serve hot.

Chicken Kufta in Yogurt Dill Broth

Prompted by Madzoon Kufta (page 116) and its traditional pairing with chicken, I fashioned this dish with chicken for the meatballs, added mustard in the broth, and baby green beans to brighten the composition. It's somewhat outlandish, but in the Armenian vein!

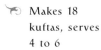 Makes 18 kuftas, serves 4 to 6

Kufta

½ cup medium bulgur

½ pound boneless, skinless chicken breast, cut into
   1-inch cubes

½ teaspoon ground coriander

1 teaspoon salt

¾ teaspoon Aleppo pepper

Yogurt Dill Broth

4 cups low-sodium chicken broth

1 teaspoon salt

2 cups yogurt

1 large egg

1 tablespoon chopped fresh dill

1 tablespoon Dijon mustard

Recipe continues on next page

Garnishes

¼ pound haricots verts or small green beans
2 tablespoons chopped fresh flat-leaf parsley
Hot paprika

Soak the bulgur in water to cover for 15 minutes. Drain and transfer to a bowl. Mince the chicken as finely as possible in a food processor. Add to the bulgur, along with the coriander, salt, and Aleppo pepper, and knead to mix. Set aside in the refrigerator for 30 minutes, or up to several hours. Form into 1½-inch balls and refrigerate until ready to cook.

In a saucepan, bring the broth and salt to a boil over high heat. Gently drop in the kuftas and decrease the heat to maintain a brisk simmer. Cover and cook until the kuftas rise up and are firm, about 6 minutes.

Meanwhile, cook the green beans in lightly salted boiling water until al dente, 5 to 8 minutes, depending on the size of the beans. Drain and set aside.

To serve, whisk together the yogurt, egg, dill, and mustard in a bowl. Whisk in a little of the poaching broth, then stir the mixture into the pot with the kuftas. Ladle the kuftas and broth into wide soup bowls. Garnish with the green beans, parsley, and a sprinkle of paprika. Serve hot.

Whitefish Kuftas

These delicate fish balls can be served as an appetizer simply garnished with lemon wedges. Or, for a salad opener to a formal meal, I like to set them on a bed of frisée or watercress sprigs and drizzle them with Lemony Homemade Mayonnaise (page 120).

Makes 24 kuftas, serves 8

½ cup medium bulgur
¾ pound white-fish fillets, such as sea bass or halibut,
    cut into 2-inch chunks
½ teaspoon chopped fresh tarragon leaves
2 teaspoons chopped lemon zest
1 teaspoon kosher salt
½ teaspoon Aleppo pepper
¼ cup extra virgin olive oil
Lemon wedges or Lemony Homemade Mayonnaise
    (page 120), for serving

Soak the bulgur in water to cover for 15 minutes. Drain and transfer to a food processor. Add the fish, tarragon, zest, salt, and Aleppo pepper to the processor and puree finely. Divide the mixture into 24 portions, roll each into a ball, then flatten the ball slightly. Place on a plate as you go. Refrigerate the kuftas to chill and firm for 30 minutes, or up to 1 hour.

To cook the kuftas, heat the olive oil in a large sauté pan over medium heat. Add the kuftas and cook, turning them around occasionally, for 5 minutes, until golden all around. Transfer to a platter, garnish with the lemon wedges, and serve warm or at room temperature.

LEMONY HOMEMADE MAYONNAISE

I use the whole egg, not just the yolk, because the white helps bind the mayonnaise without having to add another binder such as mustard.

> 1 large egg
> 2 tablespoons freshly squeezed lemon juice
> ½ teaspoon kosher salt
> 1 cup extra virgin olive oil
> 2 tablespoons water, if necessary

Blend together the egg, lemon juice, and salt in a food processor or blender. With the motor running, gradually add the oil in a thin stream to make a thin emulsion. If necessary, add a little water to make the mayonnaise thin enough to pour in a thick stream. Use right away or store in the refrigerator for up to 5 days.

Butter Kufta with Tomato and Green Bell Pepper
Yala Kufta

Armenians love butter almost as much as the French and Swiss do. It is stirred into yogurt soups, slathered on layers of savory and sweet fillo pastries, and even used to bind a vegetarian kufta. It's important to use fine bulgur, otherwise the kufta will be crumbly. Yala kufta is uncooked, like Chee Kufta (page 104), and served as a maza. To simplify, you can spread the kufta mix on a platter without forming it into balls and dollop the yogurt garnish around the edge.

Makes 12 kuftas, serves 8 to 10

1 cup fine bulgur

1 medium tomato, peeled, seeded, and finely chopped

2 tablespoons finely chopped yellow or white onion

1 scallion, white and light green part, finely chopped

2 tablespoons chopped fresh flat-leaf parsley

2 tablespoons finely chopped green bell pepper

1 teaspoon kosher salt

½ teaspoon Aleppo pepper

3 tablespoons butter, at room temperature

Garnish

½ cup yogurt

2 tablespoons chopped fresh flat-leaf parsley

1 scallion, white and light green part, finely chopped

Kosher salt

Combine the bulgur and tomato in a bowl and set aside for 15 minutes. Add the remaining ingredients and knead to blend well. Refrigerate for 30 minutes to chill and firm.

Stir together the yogurt, parsley, scallion, and salt to taste and set aside.

Form the kufta mixture into 1-inch balls and arrange on a serving platter. Garnish each kufta with a dollop of the yogurt sauce and serve.

Red Lentil Kufta

Vosbov Kufta

Reminiscent of Indian dal dishes or Greek yellow lentil fritters (vos means lentils in Armenian), here lentils are used to make Lenten kuftas, when one must eschew meat and satisfy taste in other ways. I discovered them when I was writing this book—we didn't have them in my family—they're one of my favorite kuftas.

½ cup red lentils

1½ cups water

6 tablespoons butter

½ large yellow or white onion, finely chopped

½ cup medium bulgur

¼ large green bell pepper, finely chopped

2 scallions, white and light green part, finely chopped

2 tablespoons finely chopped fresh flat-leaf parsley

½ teaspoon kosher salt

½ teaspoon Aleppo pepper

Garnishes

2 tablespoons chopped fresh flat-leaf parsley

Paprika, hot or mild, according to taste

2 tablespoons extra virgin olive oil

Cook the lentils in boiling salted water over medium-high heat for 20 minutes, until soft and almost dry but still a little moist. Transfer to a bowl.

Makes 20 kuftas, serves 10 to 12

While the lentils cook, melt the butter in a frying pan over medium heat. Stir in the onion and cook, stirring occasionally, for 5 minutes, until the onion is soft. Add to the bowl with the lentils, along with the bulgur, bell pepper, scallion, parsley, salt, and Aleppo pepper. Mix and knead until well combined. Chill for 30 minutes.

Roll the lentil mixture into 20 walnut-size balls. Chill for 30 minutes, or up to several hours, to firm.

To serve, arrange the kuftas on a platter. Sprinkle with the parsley and some paprika. Drizzle the olive oil over all and serve right away.

Chickpea Kufta with Pine Nut Filling

Chickpea kuftas are like an Armenian falafel with a nugget of savory goodness in the center. Fastidious cooks peel the chickpeas after cooking for a smoother texture, but I don't bother. I do always, however, cook the chickpeas myself. These kuftas are best served shortly after cooking—they lose their sparky flavor if kept overnight.

Makes 12 to 14 kuftas, serves 6 to 8

¾ cup fine or medium bulgur

¾ cup water

2 cups cooked chickpeas (page 35), drained and patted dry

½ medium yellow or white onion, finely chopped

¼ cup cilantro leaves, finely chopped

½ teaspoon Aleppo pepper

½ teaspoon kosher salt

Filling

1 tablespoon butter

3 tablespoons finely chopped yellow or white onion

2 tablespoons pine nuts

2 tablespoons chopped cilantro leaves

½ teaspoon ground cumin

½ teaspoon kosher salt

¼ teaspoon Aleppo pepper

1 cup yogurt, drained for 15 minutes, and whisked smooth, for serving

"Meat"balls: Kufta • 125

In a bowl, combine the bulgur and water and set aside to soak for 15 minutes. Drain and shake dry.

In a food processor, puree the bulgur, chickpeas, onion, cilantro, Aleppo pepper, and salt for 1 minute, until thick and well blended. Set aside in the refrigerator until chilled and firm, about 45 minutes.

To make the filling, melt the butter in a sauté pan over medium heat. Stir in the onion and cook for 2 minutes, until well wilted. Stir in the pine nuts, cilantro, cumin, salt, and Aleppo pepper. Remove from the heat and set aside to cool.

Bring a large pot of salted water to a boil. Form the chickpea mixture into 2-inch balls. Poke a hole in the center of each ball, fill with about 1 teaspoon of the pine nut filling, pinch closed, and roll between your palms to seal any cracks. Set aside on a plate.

To cook the kuftas, gently lower the balls into the boiling water, decrease the heat to maintain a brisk simmer, and poach, uncovered, until cooked and floating to the top, about 10 minutes. With a wire strainer or slotted spoon, lift out the kuftas and place them on paper towels to drain briefly. Serve warm, with the yogurt on the side.

Potato and Chickpea Fritters

Not all kuftas are round. Sautéed in butter, this pureed potato and chickpea mix is shaped into patties, fritter-style. Serve them before or alongside any meal.

Makes 12
patties

1 large (about 1 pound) russet potato, peeled and cut
    into 2-inch chunks
1 cup cooked chickpeas (page 35), drained
1 tablespoon tahini paste
1 teaspoon salt
¼ cup water
2 tablespoons extra-virgin olive oil, for frying
½ cup Chaiman Paste (page 44), for serving
12 sprigs cilantro, for serving

Boil the potato in a large pot of salted water until tender but not disintegrating, 10 to 12 minutes. Drain and set aside to cool until no longer steaming.

Combine the potato, chickpeas, tahini paste, salt, and water in a food processor and puree. Form the mixture into patties about 3 inches across and ½ inch thick.

Heat the oil in a large sauté pan over medium-high heat until sizzling. Add as many patties as will fit without crowding and sauté, turning once, until golden on both sides, about 5 minutes altogether. Transfer to a serving platter and continue with another round until all the patties are fried.

Place a dab of chaiman paste and a cilantro sprig on top of each patty and serve warm.

Lamb and Other Meats

❖

Lamb is the signature meat of Armenian cuisine. It appears ground for meatballs, as whole leg or whole beast, in kebab chunks for grilling, as shanks for braising, and as riblets to add a meat element to vegetable stews. The lamb we often find in markets today is imported from New Zealand or Australia and is of excellent quality. It has a gamier taste than the softer-on-the tongue meat of American lamb, more akin, in my imagination, to the taste Armenians in the Old World favored. Ironically, it's usually less expensive than domestic lamb and more available. Ironically, too, my father preferred American lamb; he was a consummate man of his New World. For myself, the imported meat shows off the traditional flavors of these wonderful dishes.

Pork is by and large not a part of Armenian food (a culinary characteristic shared with the Persians, Greeks, and Turks), even though it is not prohibited by the dietary laws of the Armenian Orthodox Church. Perhaps the scarcity of pork dishes is a result of centuries of living in the midst of Islamic cultures: Armenians simply didn't acquire a taste for the meat. Curiously, in their new country, even when there were plenty of pigs available from American farms and no influencing population nearby that proscribed eating pork, Armenian cuisine never whole-heartedly adopted it. Nonetheless, there are representational pork dishes, and I include two special favorites, Pork Shish Kebab (page 136) and a meat and apricot stew (page 146) in this chapter.

Beef, however, is another story. Its rarity in the early Armenian reper-toire was probably due to its scarcity rather than to religious proscription. When they found themselves in proximity to the Great American Plains and the West, with its vast expanses of grazing land and abundance of beef at an affordable price, Armenians were quick to swap lamb for beef in many traditional dishes, to the extent of sometimes preferring beef for dolmas.

Shish Kebab: Art and Soul

Serves 8

For me, shish kebab signifies the art and soul of my father, and my connection to the Armenian side of my family. When I was growing up, shish kebab was Dad's big deal. We had it every time there was a celebration: Easter; someone's birthday; getting together with the non-Armenian relatives from New Mexico; a beautiful day in the backyard.

Dad had some serious, de rigueur guidelines about the shish kebab. First of all, the shishes (skewers) were made of metal. They were hand-forged in a square so the meat chunks wouldn't twirl about as they would if the skewers were round. The metal also assured the meat would be heated from the inside as the skewers got hot over the fire. These shishes were part of our household, carried along wherever we traveled.

Just as important, nothing but his own boned-out, perfectly uniform, hand-cut leg of lamb squares would do. The vegetables—onions, green bell peppers, and tomatoes—had to be whole and skewered exactly through the middle so they, too, would stay put without twirling as the shishes were turned on the grill. No cutting the vegetables into chunks and no marinade for the meat. That was for other Armenians, not him.

As it finished cooking, each vegetable or meat was pushed off its skewer into a large pot using a chunk of bread as a hot pad and set aside, without being tossed or stirred, to quietly mingle aroma and juices until all the shishes had been cooked. Then the whole pot was served, just like that, with an accompanying pot of rice pilaf.

Here's the recipe for how we did the shish kebab when I was a kid, plus an optional marinade for those who, like me, like a little extra seasoning in the meat. For his shish kebab feasts, Dad always allowed 1 whole bell pepper, 1 whole tomato, and 3 onions per person. That's generous; you could stretch it a bit further.

1 leg of lamb (about 4½ pounds)

Aintab or Marash Marinade (optional, see box, page 133)

Salt and freshly ground black pepper

8 whole green bell peppers

16 whole boiling onions, peeled

8 whole ripe tomatoes

2 recipes Basic Rice Pilaf (page 250), warm, for serving

2 recipes Yogurt with Cucumber (page 21), for serving

Bone the lamb (or have the butcher do it), reserving the bone. Trim the fat off the outside and cut the meat into 1½-inch cubes, trimming extra fat and gristle as you go. Reserve the trimming and bone and use for other dishes.

Place the lamb cubes in a large nonreactive dish and sprinkle with salt and pepper. Add the marinade, if using, toss to coat, and set aside at room temperature for 2 hours, or refrigerate for up to overnight. Remove from the refrigerator 30 minutes before cooking.

Prepare a medium-hot charcoal fire or preheat a gas grill to medium high. String the meat on skewers. String the vegetables on skewers, one kind of vegetable per skewer without mixing them up, because they cook for different times.

To cook the shish kebabs, place the bell pepper skewers on the grill rack directly over the coals. Cook, turning 3 or 4 times, until the peppers are charred and collapsed, 15 to 18 minutes, depending on the size. Transfer to a large pot and set aside.

Next, cook the onions the same way until you can pierce them but they are still a little crunchy, 10 to 15 minutes, depending on the size, and then the tomatoes until collapsed and slightly charred, 8 to 10 minutes. Transfer all to the pot with the peppers as they are done. Finally, cook the lamb until medium rare, rotating in one-quarter turns, about 8 minutes, and add to the vegetables. Serve with a steaming bowl of rice pilaf and the yogurt with cucumber on the side.

THE RELATIVES' AINTAB OR MARASH MARINADE

Though my dad insisted the lamb for shish kebab was best plain and simple, seasoned only with salt and pepper, many Armenians, including me and my cousin, Gary Jenanyan, prefer to toss the meat in a marinade before grilling it. Since our families came from Aintab and Marash, I call the marinade by that name, and that's how Gary and I prepared the lamb when we catered a Jenanyan family reunion in a Sacramento park in 1995. Gary, a professional chef and caterer, trucked his six-foot-long grills to the site and built a magnificent mesquite fire in each. When the fires were just right, coals covered with white ash with some red glowing through, we strung the marinated meat on shishes, and, with my husband, Rick, also manning the grill, cooked it just like we had learned growing up. The relatives, one hundred strong, were ecstatic that any of our generation knew the right seasonings and techniques, and a happy, nostalgic time was had by all. We called it an Armenian re-evolution! The marinade also makes an excellent soak for lamb chops.

To prepare enough marinade for 8 servings, combine ¼ cup extra virgin olive oil, 1 tablespoon freshly squeezed lemon juice, 2 tablespoons coarsely grated yellow onion, 1 teaspoon chopped fresh oregano (or ½ teaspoon dried oregano), 1 teaspoon kosher salt, and ½ teaspoon Aleppo pepper and whisk to mix.

Pour over the lamb cubes, toss to coat, and set aside to marinate at room temperature for at least 2 hours, or marinate in the refrigerator overnight.

Beef Shish Kebab
Basterma Shaslik

Serve 4 to 6

Shish kebabs of beef lightly marinated in red wine vinegar are a well-known spe-cialty of Caucasian Armenians. I like to include a California touch with pasilla or Anaheim chili pepper squares in the marinade to give a bite to the whole bit. Skewers of tomato often accompany the beef.

1½ pounds boneless top sirloin, cut into 1½-inch cubes
Kosher salt and freshly ground black pepper
2 tablespoons extra virgin olive oil
1 tablespoon red wine vinegar
1 small yellow or white onion, cut into 1-inch squares
2 medium fresh pasilla or Anaheim chiles, stemmed,
    seeded, membranes removed, and cut into 1-inch
    squares
24 cherry tomatoes (optional)

Place the meat in a dish large enough to hold the cubes in one layer. Sprin-kle liberally with salt and pepper. Add the oil, vinegar, onion, and chili peppers and toss to coat the meat. Set aside to marinate at room temper-ature for 2 hours or marinate in the refrigerator for up to 4 hours, remov-ing 30 minutes before cooking.

Prepare a medium-hot charcoal fire or preheat a gas grill to medium high. Skewer the meat cubes alternately with 2 or 3 each of the onion and pepper squares. String the tomatoes, if using, on separate skewers.

Place the meat skewers on the grill rack directly over the heat and cook, rotating in one-quarter turns, for 8 minutes, until medium rare. Transfer to a platter and let rest for 5 minutes for the juices to settle. Add the tomatoes, if using, to the grill and cook, turning once, for 4 to 5 minutes, until soft and lightly charred. Add to the platter and serve right away.

Pork Shish Kebab in Pomegranate, Sumac, and Black Pepper Marinade

Serves 4 to 6

Here, pork puts in one of its infrequent appearances on the Armenian table in an out-of-the-ordinary shish kebab. In the marinade, which turns into a sauce, sumac lends its exotic glow and subtly tangy taste that is doubled with tart, red-orange pomegranate molasses. A nice accompaniment is grilled green and red bell pepper squares, skewered separately and grilled al dente (about 10 minutes).

Note: Be sure to marinate the meat no longer than an hour or the marinade will overwhelm it.

Marinade

4 tablespoons pomegranate molasses

4 tablespoons white wine

1 clove garlic, minced or pressed

¼ teaspoon cracked black peppercorns

¼ teaspoon kosher salt

½ teaspoon ground sumac

1 tablespoon extra virgin olive oil

1½ pounds boneless country-style pork ribs,
    cut into 1½- to 2-inch cubes

Combine the ingredients for the marinade in a dish large enough to hold the pork cubes in one packed layer. Add the cubes and toss to coat. Set aside in the refrigerator to marinate for 45 minutes to 1 hour.

Prepare a medium-hot charcoal fire or preheat a gas grill to medium high. String the pork onto skewers, reserving the marinade. Grill the kebabs over indirect heat, covered, for 20 to 30 minutes, turning 3 or 4 times, until nicely charred on the outside and no longer pink in the center. Transfer to a serving platter and let sit for 5 minutes for the juices to settle.

While the kebabs rest, reduce the marinade in a small saucepan over medium-high heat until thick and bubbly, 2 to 3 minutes. Serve the kebabs with the reduced marinade on the side.

Butterflied Leg of Lamb Marinated in Mint Sumac Vinaigrette

Serves 8

In a variation on the Armenian theme of pairing lamb with mint and lemon, champagne vinegar replaces the citrus, and sumac adds its woodsy astringency to the marinade. It's a delightful dish for any special occasion when the weather allows grilling.

¼ cup chopped fresh mint leaves

½ teaspoon ground sumac

2 cloves garlic, minced or pressed

¼ cup champagne vinegar

½ cup extra virgin olive oil

½ teaspoon kosher salt

1 teaspoon freshly ground black pepper

1 leg of lamb, butterflied

Combine all the ingredients except the lamb in a dish large enough to hold the lamb spread out. Add the lamb and turn to coat. Set aside in the refrigerator to marinate at least 6 hours or up to overnight, turning once. Remove from the refrigerator 30 minutes before cooking.

Prepare a medium-hot charcoal fire or preheat a gas grill to medium high.

Lift the lamb out of the marinade, reserving the marinade for basting, and place on the grill rack directly over the heat. Grill, turning and basting every 5 minutes or so, until medium rare, 30 to 35 minutes. Transfer to a platter and let sit in a warm place for 10 minutes for the juices to settle. Slice and serve.

Braised Lamb Shanks with White Beans and Fennel

Braising lamb shanks with wine and fennel is a California-Armenian innovation inspired by my exuberant backyard stand of fennel, which has taken over a corner of the garden. I let it grow because I enjoy the anise swallowtail butterflies it attracts to lay their eggs on fennel plants; I cut its flowers for the house, and I use its fronds and bulbs in salads, soups, and this lamb and white bean braise.

Serves 4 to 6

1½ cups dried white beans, such as Great Northerns,
    white cannelini, or flageolets
3 tablespoons extra virgin olive oil
4 small (¾ to 1 pound) lamb shanks,
    cracked in half
6 cloves garlic, minced
1 carrot, finely chopped
½ large fennel bulb, finely chopped
2 cups chopped fresh or canned tomatoes
1 bay leaf
1 cup white wine
3 cups low-sodium chicken broth
1 teaspoon hot paprika
1 teaspoon kosher salt
½ teaspoon Aleppo pepper or ⅛ teaspoon cayenne
¼ cup chopped fennel fronds or fresh flat-leaf parsley,
    for garnish

To prepare the beans, soak them overnight. Or, place them in a pot with water to cover, bring to a boil over high heat, turn off the heat, and let sit 1 hour.

In a heavy pot large enough to hold the shanks in one packed layer (use two pots if necessary), heat the oil over medium-high heat. In uncrowded batches, brown the shanks all around, then transfer them to a plate. Set aside.

Stir the garlic, carrot, and fennel into the pot, then add the tomatoes, bay leaf, wine, broth, paprika, salt, and Aleppo pepper and stir to mix. Return the lamb and collected juices to the pot and bring to a boil over high heat. Decrease the heat to medium, cover the pot, and cook for 45 minutes.

Drain the beans and stir them into the lamb. Cover again and continue cooking for 1½ hours, until the beans are tender and the lamb is falling away from the bone. Remove from the heat and let rest for 10 minutes.

To serve, remove the bay leaf and transfer the lamb, beans, vegetables, and juices to a platter or individual plates. Sprinkle the chopped fennel fronds over the top and serve.

Lamb Stew with Green Beans and Tomatoes
Fasulya

All around the Mediterranean and north to the Caucasus, lamb is paired with green beans and tomatoes in a rustic potage that serves as filling, but special, family fare. Fasulya was certain to appear on the table a few days after a leg of lamb, usually as shish kebab, was on the menu because the bones and trim provided material for the broth. Lamb neck or bone-in lamb stew meat substitute perfectly for the leg trim, and I prefer those cuts to boneless lamb stew meat because they're more tender and also because they reflect the nature of the dish as I had it growing up—an economical and tasty way to employ the bone and trim from a leg of lamb. The green beans are cooked all the way through until soft, not al dente or squeaky, but for the best flavor, they should be fresh and young to start with, or ones you've fresh-frozen yourself from the garden or farmers' market. Pilaf and yogurt with cucumber are must-have accompaniments.

Serves 6

Note: Fasulya can also be made vegetarian. Omit the meat and cook the stew for 30 to 45 minutes only. For vegetable variation ideas, see the box following recipe.

❖

2 tablespoons extra virgin olive oil

2 pounds bone-in lamb stew meat

1 medium yellow or white onion, halved and thinly sliced

2 large cloves garlic, coarsely chopped

2 large fresh tomatoes, peeled and seeded, or 2 cups
    canned tomatoes, coarsely chopped

2 teaspoons chopped fresh oregano leaves or 1 teaspoon
    dried oregano

1½ teaspoons kosher salt

¾ teaspoon Aleppo pepper

1 tablespoon tomato paste

2–3 cups water

1 pound fresh haricots verts, stems pinched off,
    beans left whole, or young, regular green beans, stems
    pinched off, beans halved lengthwise, then crosswise

¼ cup chopped fresh flat-leaf parsley, for serving

Basic Rice Pilaf (page 250), warm, for serving

Yogurt with Cucumber (page 21), for serving

Heat the oil in a large pot or pressure cooker over medium-high heat. In batches, so as not to crowd the pieces, brown the lamb all around, about 3 minutes. Transfer to a plate and continue with another batch until all the pieces are browned. Return the lamb and collected juices to the pot and add the onion and garlic. Sauté until the onion is wilted, about 2 minutes. Stir in the tomatoes, oregano, salt, Aleppo pepper, tomato paste, and 2 cups of water if pressure-cooking or 3 cups of water if simmering.

To pressure cook: Add the green beans now, lock on the lid, and bring to pressure over high heat, about 5 minutes. Decrease the heat to medium and cook for 10 minutes.

To cook on the stove top: Bring to a boil over high heat. Decrease the heat to maintain a simmer, cover, and cook for 1 hour, until the lamb is tender. Stir in the green beans and continue simmering, partially covered, for 30 minutes, until the meat is falling off the bones and the green beans are thoroughly tender.

Either way, remove from the heat and let rest for 10 minutes, or up to 1 hour, reheating if necessary.

To serve, ladle the stew into individual bowls, garnish with the parsley, and serve with the pilaf and yogurt with cucumber in separate side dishes.

LAMB AND VEGETABLE STEWS: AN ARMENIAN SPECIALTY

As well as green beans, many other vegetables frequently star in lamb stews. Try:

Cauliflower, in florets

Eggplant, in unpeeled 1-inch cubes

Zucchini, in ½-inch rounds

Okra, prepared as on page 225

Artichokes, baby ones, trimmed and halved

Leeks, white and light green parts, cut into 1-inch lengths

Ragout of Lamb with Spinach, Green Pepper, and Lentils

Serves 4 to 6

Spinach acts as both herb and vegetable, and Anaheim pepper, with its mild heat, adds punch to a favorite Armenian ragout of lamb and lentils. Unlike many ragouts that benefit from resting several hours, this one should be served soon after cooking. It becomes mushy and its fresh flavor and sparkly color fade over time.

2 tablespoons butter
2 pounds bone-in lamb stew meat
Kosher salt and freshly ground black pepper
1 yellow or white onion, finely chopped
1 Anaheim chile pepper, halved lengthwise, seeded,
    and cut into ¼-inch-wide strips
2 cups water
1 tablespoon tomato paste
1 cup French green lentils
1 bunch (about ¾ pound) spinach, including tender
    stems and roots, leaves cut crosswise into
    1-inch-wide strips (6 packed cups)
2 tablespoons freshly squeezed lemon juice

Melt the butter in a large pot over medium-high heat. Sprinkle the lamb pieces with salt and pepper and brown them in uncrowded batches, about 4 minutes per batch. (Decrease the heat to medium if the butter starts to burn.) Transfer to a plate. Add the onion and chile pepper to the pot and cook until the onion is wilted, about 2 minutes. Increase the heat to high and add the water and tomato paste. Stir to mix and bring to a boil. Return the lamb and collected juices to the pot, cover, and cook at a brisk simmer for 1 hour.

Add the lentils to the pot and stir to mix. Add the spinach and, without stirring, cover and continue simmering until the lentils are tender, about 30 minutes. Remove from the heat and let rest for 10 to 15 minutes.

To serve, reheat over medium heat, stir in the lemon juice, and serve hot.

Ragout of Lamb or Pork with Dried Apricots and Whole Garlic Cloves

I discovered the delightful combination of dried apricots and garlic many years ago at my Pig-by-the-Tail delicatessen, when it suddenly occurred to me one day to use them together as a stuffing for a boneless pork loin roast to slice and serve as a fresh cold cut. I think the flavor merger of apricot and garlic must have come out of some ancient taste, bred in my bone, which I rediscovered when preparing this book. Here it resurfaces in an elegant stew Armenians would more likely make with lamb, but, recalling that "new" discovery, I often make with pork.

> 1¼ pounds boneless lamb stew meat or
>   country-style boneless pork ribs, cut into
>   1½-inch cubes
> 1½ teaspoons kosher salt
> 2 tablespoons extra virgin olive oil
> ¼ cup brandy
> 1½ teaspoons ground cumin
> ¾ teaspoon Aleppo pepper
> 3 cups water
> 24 dried apricot halves
> 12 cloves garlic, peeled and left whole
> 2 tablespoons freshly squeezed lemon juice
> ½ cup cilantro leaves, for serving

In a bowl, toss the meat with the salt. Heat the oil in a large pot over medium-high heat. In batches, so as not to crowd the pieces, brown the meat all around, about 4 minutes. Transfer to a plate and continue until all the pieces are browned. After the last batch, return the meat and collected juices to the pot and add the brandy. Stir in the cumin, pepper, and water and bring to a boil over high heat. Decrease the heat to maintain a simmer, cover, and cook for 1 hour, until the meat is almost tender.

Skim the liquid, then stir in the apricots and garlic. Continue simmering, covered, for 30 minutes, until the meat is fork tender. Stir in the lemon juice, sprinkle the cilantro over the top, and serve right away.

Armenian Moussaka with Lamb or Beef, Potato, and Yogurt Béchamel

Moussaka, though mostly known as the famous Greek dish of eggplant layered with ground lamb or beef and béchamel, doesn't always include eggplant. It might feature potato instead, moistened and made supple with a creamy yogurt béchamel sauce. It's a wonderful small-family dish that, for a crowd, can easily be doubled or tripled and cooked in a larger dish.

Serves 4

¼ cup extra virgin olive oil

1½ pounds red, white, or Yukon gold potatoes, scrubbed and sliced ¼ inch thick

Kosher salt

1 small yellow or white onion, finely chopped

½ pound ground lamb

2 small tomatoes, peeled, seeded, and chopped

2 tablespoons chopped fresh flat-leaf parsley

1 teaspoon chopped fresh dill

¼ teaspoon ground allspice

¼ teaspoon freshly ground black pepper

1½ cups Yogurt Béchamel (page 27)

1 large egg

⅓ cup coarsely grated ricotta salata or Parmesan cheese

Preheat the oven to 350°F.

Heat the oil in a large sauté pan over medium-high heat. In batches, salt the potato slices and fry them, turning once, until just beginning to turn golden around the edges, about 3 minutes. Lift out the slices with kitchen tongs, letting excess oil drip back into the pan, and transfer to a plate.

When the last batch of potato slices is done, add the onion and lamb to the pan and sauté, stirring to break up the lamb chunks, until the lamb is no longer pink, about 2 minutes. Add the tomatoes, parsley, dill, allspice, and pepper and stir to mix. Sauté, still over medium-high heat, until the mixture is fairly dry and crumbly, 2 to 3 minutes. Remove from the heat.

To assemble and cook the dish, arrange half of the potato slices in an overlapping layer in an 8 × 10-inch casserole dish. Spread the lamb mixture over the potatoes. Cover with the remaining potato slices in an overlapping layer. Whisk the egg into the béchamel and pour over the top. Sprinkle the cheese over all. Place in the oven and bake until golden on the top and slightly brown around the edges, about 45 minutes. Remove from the oven and let rest for 15 minutes. Cut into portions and serve warm.

Lamb and Potato Fillo Pie with Pine Nuts, Raisins, and Orange Zest

Adding the potato to this Armenian meat pie was my husband Rick's idea. Being one who likes a well-rounded, hearty meal and loves casseroles, he thought the potato would add texture and richness. He was right. It's a full-up casserole pie that makes a filling family meal at the end of a yeoman's, or yeowoman's, day. The filling can be used for many other purposes, such as filling individual boereks or, especially good, as stuffing for green bell pepper or tomato dolmas.

Makes one 9 × 9-inch pie; serves 4 as an entrée

Filling

1 potato, red, white, or Yukon gold, scrubbed and cut
     into ¼-inch dice
1 tablespoon butter
½ pound lean ground lamb
1 medium yellow or white onion, finely chopped
3 tablespoons pine nuts
¼ cup raisins
1 teaspoon finely chopped orange zest
1 teaspoon finely chopped fresh mint leaves
¼ teaspoon ground allspice
Tiny pinch of cinnamon
1 teaspoon kosher salt
½ teaspoon freshly ground black pepper
1 large egg, lightly beaten

4 tablespoons (½ stick) melted butter, for brushing the fillo
12 (8 × 13-inch) sheets fillo dough

To make the filling, place the potatoes in a small saucepan, add water to cover by 1 inch, and bring to a boil over high heat. Cook until the potatoes can be pierced but are still al dente, about 4 minutes. Drain in a colander and set aside.

Melt the butter in a sauté pan over medium-high heat. Add the lamb and cook, using a fork to stir and break up the chunks, until crumbly and no longer pink, about 3 minutes. Add the onion, pine nuts, and raisins and continue cooking for 3 minutes, until the onion is well wilted. Add the zest, mint, allspice, cinnamon, salt, pepper, and potatoes and stir to mix. Remove from the heat and stir in the egg. Set aside to cool.

To make the pie, preheat the oven to 350°F. Lightly grease a 9 × 9-inch baking dish with a little of the melted butter.

Lay 2 fillo sheets in the bottom of the dish and brush the top sheet with butter. (The fillo sheets will edge up the sides of the dish.) Place 2 more sheets on top and brush with butter again. Top with 2 more sheets of fillo and brush with butter. Spread the filling over the fillo. Cover with 2 more sheets of fillo, brush with butter, then 2 more, brush with butter, then 2 more sheets. Finally, brush the top with butter.

Bake until golden and crispy, about 35 minutes. Cut into portions and serve warm.

Grilled Lamb Hearts with Parsley Sauce

Serves 6

In Armenian cuisine, no part of the lamb, from head to tail, goes uncooked. The lamb's heart is a special delicacy I love for its rich flavor, lean meat, and firm texture that takes to many seasonings. The parsley sauce is a superb accompaniment that can also be used with grilled rabbit, sausage, lamb chops, and vegetables, such as zucchini, tomatoes, and potatoes.

Note: Lamb hearts, though not widely available, can be found in butcher stores that cater to the adventuresome cook.

Parsley Sauce

    1 cup chopped fresh flat-leaf parsley
    2 teaspoons chopped fresh oregano
    2 large garlic cloves, finely chopped
    ½ cup extra virgin olive oil
    ½ teaspoon kosher salt
    ½ teaspoon freshly ground black pepper

    4 lamb hearts (6 to 8 ounces each)
    Lemon wedges, for garnish

To make the parsley sauce, mix together all the ingredients in a small bowl.

Slit the lamb hearts open, slicing down the center enough to butterfly them without cutting them all the way in half. Place them in a dish large enough to hold them opened out. Add ¼ cup of the parsley sauce, turn to coat, and set aside to marinate for 30 minutes at room temperature, or up to several hours in the refrigerator.

When ready to cook, prepare a medium-hot charcoal fire or preheat a gas grill to medium high.

Place the hearts on the grill rack directly above the coals and cook, turning once, for 15 to 20 minutes, until medium rare.

Transfer the hearts to a serving platter and drizzle about ¼ cup of the remaining sauce over the top. Garnish with the lemon wedges and serve right away, with the remaining sauce on the side.

Poultry, Game, and Eggs

❖

When I was growing up, husbanding poultry and rabbits and hunting game were part of providing for the table. This was men's work, and my Uncle Whitey did both ably. He was not at all Armenian, but married into the family via Aunt Rose, my father's sister. He earned a living as a railroad conductor. At home, he maintained a backyard coop with chickens and Chinese ring-necked pheasants, which, strangely, wouldn't sit on their eggs, so the chicken hens did the job. Once, when for some reason I cannot remember, he took some of us kids to the San Francisco zoo, I learned that

Uncle Whitey, Aunt Rose's husband, this time with fish for the table.

camels love to chew cigarettes, and free-range peacocks can be approached close enough to have a feather plucked for festooning a child's desk. When the peacock feather eventually got worn and dusty, I left it by the wayside, but I am quite sure I will forever cherish the experience of getting close enough to a wild animal to feed it or borrow one of its feathers, and of eating truly fresh home-grown chicken and eggs. This chapter's recipes were inspired by such memories, and the Armenian traditions for preparing poultry, game, and eggs.

Armenian Stewed Chicken

🐑 Serves 6 to 8

In a stew that evokes Caucasian-Armenian cooking, chicken and homey root vegetables are combined in a healthy, warming dish made bright with a generous amount of fresh herbs both in the broth and as garnish. Don't be put off by the long list of ingredients, this is a simple, one-pot preparation.

1 (5- to 6-pound) roasting chicken , cut up, or the same
    amount of chicken pieces
1 small celery root, peeled and cut into 1-inch cubes
18 boiling onions, peeled
3 sprigs mint
6 sprigs flat-leaf parsley
4 tablespoons butter
5 cups low-sodium chicken broth
5 cups water
1½ teaspoons kosher salt
½ teaspoon freshly ground black pepper
16 baby carrots, peeled, or 4 large carrots, peeled and
    cut into 1-inch rounds
16 fingerling or creamer-size Yukon gold potatoes

1 tablespoon chopped fresh mint leaves
¼ cup chopped fresh flat-leaf parsley
3 cups yogurt

Place the chicken, celery root, onion, mint sprigs, parsley sprigs, butter, broth, water, salt, and pepper in a large soup pot. Bring to a boil, skimming from time to time. Decrease the heat to maintain a simmer, partially cover the pot, and cook for 45 minutes, until the vegetables are almost, but not quite, fork tender. Add the carrots and potatoes and continue simmering uncovered for 20 minutes more, until the chicken and all the vegetables are fork tender and the liquid is golden and brothy.

With a wire strainer, transfer the chicken and vegetables to a platter, reserving the broth (see below). Sprinkle the chopped herbs over the platter and serve with the yogurt on the side.

EASY ARMENIAN CHICKEN RICE SOUP

Strain the reserved broth from cooking the chicken and let it cool completely. Cover and refrigerate overnight. The next day, skim off the fat. Reheat the broth with any chicken or vegetables left over from the stew (cut into small dice), 1 cup of cooked rice, and a large pinch of paprika. Serve hot.

Stewed Chicken in Lemon and Egg Sauce with Roasted Onions and Carrots

Serves 4

The chicken and egg come together in this classic pan-Armenian preparation. It's one of the easiest elegant dishes I know, and requires few ingredients. I use skinned chicken because it makes for a clearer, more pristine sauce-on-the-spot. To remove the skin, use a paper towel to hold a chicken piece in one hand and, holding another paper towel in the other hand, grasp the skin and pull it off.

1 chicken (3½ to 4 pounds) cut into pieces and skinned
3 cups low-sodium chicken broth
1 teaspoon kosher salt
3 egg yolks, beaten
⅓ cup freshly squeezed lemon juice

Roasted Onions and Carrots

1 large yellow or white onion, halved and sliced
    ½ inch thick
3 carrots, cut into ½-inch-thick, 2-inch-long sticks
1 tablespoons extra virgin olive oil
Kosher salt and Aleppo pepper

½ cup chopped fresh flat-leaf parsley, for serving

In a large pot, combine the chicken, broth, and salt and bring to a boil over high heat. Decrease the heat to maintain a simmer, partially cover, and cook for 20 minutes, until the chicken is just tender and no longer pink (the pieces will continue to cook as they rest while the sauce is made). Transfer the pieces to a plate and set aside in a warm place. Reserve the liquid in the pot.

While the chicken cooks, prepare the roasted vegetables. Preheat the oven to 375°F. Place the onion slices and carrot sticks on a baking sheet. Toss with the olive oil and a liberal sprinkling of salt and Aleppo pepper. Place in the oven and roast for 25 minutes, until ever-so-slightly charred. Remove and set aside in a warm place for a few minutes while preparing the sauce.

To prepare the sauce, bring the liquid from cooking the chicken to a boil over medium-high heat. Decrease the heat to medium and whisk in the egg yolks and lemon juice. Cook, stirring frequently, until thickened and saucy, about 15 minutes.

To serve, return the chicken to the pot to reheat briefly. Transfer to a serving platter and surround with the roasted vegetables. Pour the sauce over all, sprinkle with the parsley, and serve.

Spring Chicken Stew with Leeks, Fava Beans, and Tarragon

Serves 4

There are two kinds of tarragon, French and Russian, both perennials. The Russian varietal has a soft aroma with just a hint of licorice, and it's the kind that's usually called for in Armenian or other Caucasian recipes. It's very easy to grow in pots or in the garden. I prefer the French varietal with its more pronounced licorice flavor that adds as much spice as verve to a dish. It too grows easily in a pot or in the ground, but don't be surprised when it dies back all the way to the ground during winter; it's not lost, just dormant until next spring. In any case, the tarragon should be fresh from the garden or, these days, a supermarket—dried tarragon is too strident. I like to use a small chicken for this stew because it divides neatly into quarters that are just the right size for four portions, and it cooks up tender in no time flat.

One small (2½- to 3-pound) chicken, quartered
1 teaspoon kosher salt
3 tablespoons butter or extra virgin olive oil
½ cup white wine
2 cups low-sodium chicken broth
1 teaspoon chopped fresh tarragon
½ teaspoon Aleppo pepper
6 small or 2 medium leeks, white and light green part,
    cut into 3- to 4-inch-long shreds, washed, and drained
4 to 5 pounds fresh fava beans in the pod, shelled,
    blanched, and peeled (page 94)
2 tablespoons chopped fresh flat-leaf parsley

Toss the chicken quarters with the salt. Melt the butter in a large sauté pan over medium-high heat. Add the chicken, skin side down, and brown lightly, about 2 minutes. Turn, decrease the heat to medium, and brown on the other side, about 2 minutes.

Add the wine, broth, tarragon, and Aleppo pepper and stir to mix. Spread the leeks over the chicken and bring to a boil over high heat. Decrease the heat to maintain a simmer, cover, and cook for 20 minutes. Turn over the chicken pieces and continue cooking, covered, until the chicken is just tender and no longer pink between the leg and thigh, about 10 minutes.

Stir in the fava beans and let heat in the stew for about 3 minutes. Correct the salt seasoning, sprinkle the parsley over the top, and serve.

Baked Chicken in Yogurt Turmeric Sauce with Fresh Peas

In this gaily-colored dish, with its blazing orange/yellow turmeric and contrasting bright green peas, I take Armenian cooking in a southerly direction, toward India, land of saffron robes and many Armenian enclaves. I recommend fresh turmeric if you can find it. A rhizome like ginger, only smaller, fresh turmeric adds a vegetable flavor, somewhat like ginger crossed with carrot, to the dish. It's available in Indian and Middle Eastern markets and produce stores that cater to an international clientele.

The sauce, uncooked and with the addition of cumin, makes an excellent dip for the maza table.

Serves 4

Sauce

1½ cups yogurt

1 tablespoon peeled and finely chopped fresh turmeric
  or 1 teaspoon ground turmeric

2 teaspoons chopped fresh dill

1 teaspoon kosher salt

1 (3½- to 4-pound) chicken, cut up, wing tips and backbone reserved for another purpose, or an equivalent
  amount of chicken pieces, skinned (page 159)

1 pound fresh peas, shelled

Bulgur and Walnut Pilaf (page 260), warm, for serving

Whisk together the sauce ingredients in a baking dish or oven casserole large enough to hold the chicken pieces without overlapping. Add the chicken and turn to coat. Set aside to marinate for 30 minutes. Or, refrigerate up to overnight (remove from the refrigerator 30 minutes before cooking).

When ready to cook, preheat the oven to 375°F.

Cover the baking dish, place in the oven, and bake for 25 minutes. Turn the pieces over and bake for 15 to 20 minutes more, depending on the size of the chicken, until the juices are golden.

While the chicken cooks, bring a small pot of water to boil over high heat. Add the peas and immediately drain in a colander. Set aside.

To serve, transfer the chicken to a platter. Stir the peas into the sauce and pour over the chicken. Serve right away, with the pilaf on the side.

GRILLED CHICKEN IN YOGURT TURMERIC SAUCE

The chicken is also delicious grilled: Prepare a medium-hot charcoal fire or preheat a gas grill to medium high. Lift the chicken pieces out of the sauce, reserving the sauce. Place the chicken on the grill rack around the heat, not directly over it, and grill for 35 to 40 minutes, turning once. Place the reserved sauce in a small saucepan, bring to a boil over medium-high heat, and simmer for a few minutes to cook the raw chicken juices. Stir in the peas, pour over the chicken, and serve.

Baked Chicken with Olives, Turnips, and Turnip Greens

I cooked a variation of this dish, made with duck rather than chicken and without the turnip greens, for the first-ever meal served at Berkeley's world-famous Chez Panisse restaurant on August 28, 1971. I don't know why I chose it for the opener, except its elements appealed to my French-cuisine style at the time, and also to my Armenian taste for turnips and olives. Dinner was rather later than advertised— we were all novices in the restaurant business—and was not quite perfect that night. I have made the dish countless times since. Adding turnip greens is one of my favorite latter-day innovations.

Serves 4 to 6

12 baby turnips, with greens, or 3 regular turnips plus
  ½ bunch fresh turnip greens
1 (3½- to 4-pound) chicken, quartered
1 small yellow or white onion, halved and thinly
  sliced
1 large tomato, cut into 1-inch wedges
1 bay leaf
1 teaspoon paprika, hot or mild
1 teaspoon kosher salt
½ teaspoon freshly ground black pepper
¾ cup white wine
1 cup (about 4 ounces) picholine or other mild green
  olives, not pitted

Preheat the oven to 350°F.

If using baby turnips, trim and scrub them, saving the greens. Cut the turnips in half and set aside. If using regular turnips, peel them and cut into ½- to ¾-inch wedges. Set aside. Thinly shred the greens, wash and drain them, and set aside.

Place the chicken, onion, tomato, bay leaf, paprika, salt, pepper, and wine in an oven dish large enough to hold the ingredients in one crowded layer. Turn to coat, winding up with the chicken skin side up. Cover and bake for 30 minutes. Turn the chicken over, and continue baking uncovered for 25 minutes, until the chicken is almost done.

Remove the cover and turn the chicken over again (skin side up again). Tuck the turnips and olives under the chicken and bake, uncovered, for 30 minutes, until the turnips are tender and the chicken is golden on top. Remove the bay leaf, stir in the turnip greens, and cook uncovered for 3 minutes more, until the greens wilt. Serve right away.

Grilled Chicken Marinated in Garlic and Olive Oil with Tahini Sauce and Grilled Figs

Serves 4 to 6

Armenians, with their love of outdoor socials, are fond of grilled chicken, usually rubbed with garlic and olive oil, for such occasions. The tahini sauce and figs are my innovation on that old theme; together, they can also complement simply grilled duck or pork.

1 (3½-pound) chicken, cut into serving pieces
2 large cloves garlic, finely chopped
¼ cup extra virgin olive oil
1 teaspoon Aleppo pepper
1 teaspoon kosher salt

Tahini Sauce

¼ cup tahini
2 large cloves garlic, cut up
¼ cup extra virgin olive oil
¼ cup freshly squeezed lemon juice
¼ cup white wine
½ teaspoon Aleppo pepper
½ teaspoon kosher salt

6 firm, fresh green figs

Place the chicken pieces in one layer in a nonreactive dish. Add the garlic, oil, Aleppo pepper, and salt and turn to coat. Set aside to marinate in the refrigerator for 1 hour.

To make the tahini sauce, combine all the ingredients in a food processor and blend into a smooth mixture with the consistency of mayonnaise. Set aside at room temperature for up to several hours, or refrigerate for up to 3 days (bring to room temperature before serving).

To cook the chicken, prepare a medium-hot charcoal fire or preheat a gas grill to medium high. Grill over indirect heat, turning occasionally, for 30 to 35 minutes, until the pieces are cooked through but still moist (the thighs will take a bit longer than the breasts). Transfer to a serving platter and set aside in a warm place for a few minutes while cooking the figs.

To cook the figs, cut them in half lengthwise. Place them directly over the heat and grill for 3 minutes, turning once, until lightly charred and softened.

To serve, arrange the figs around the chicken. Serve warm with the tahini sauce on the side.

Fried Flattened Baby Chickens or Game Hens with Quince or Tart Apples

🖙 Serves 2

Baby chickens, weighing between 2 and 2½ pounds each, used to be widely available as "broiler" chickens, and they are the ones my father preferred for their tender, sweet meat. For some reason, we rarely see them in markets these days, but game hens or the even smaller specialty-item poussins work as well. Flattening the chicken ensures that it cooks evenly, and brining it tightens the meat and skin so the skin crisps better. Quinces, which turn an attractive peachy pink and become quite fragrant when cooked, are in season for only a short time, late October to December or January. I recommend you seize the moment to make the dish with them.

Brine

3 tablespoons kosher salt

8 cups water

2 bay leaves, crumbled

2 baby chickens or game hens

4 tablespoons butter

2 quinces or tart apples, such as pippins or Granny Smiths

1 large clove garlic, finely chopped

2 tablespoons chopped fresh chives

To prepare the brine, combine the salt, water, and bay leaves in a deep dish and stir to dissolve the salt. Set aside.

Place the chickens breast side down on a cutting board and cut along each side of the backbones to remove them. Turn the chickens breast side up and pound them with a mallet to crack the breast bones and flatten the chickens. Place the chickens (one on top of the other is okay) in the brine. Cover and place in the refrigerator for 6 hours, up to overnight.

To cook the chickens, lift them out of the brine and pat them dry. Discard the brine. In a sauté pan large enough to hold both chickens flattened out (use 2 pans, if necessary), melt the butter over medium heat. Add the chickens, skin side down, decrease the heat to medium low, and cook for 15 minutes, until golden on the bottom.

While the chicken cooks on the first side, peel and core the quinces, then cut them into 1-inch wedges. (If using apples, leave them unpeeled.)

Turn over the chicken, add the quince and garlic to the pan, and stir to mix. Continue cooking for 25 minutes, until the chicken is no longer pink between the leg and thigh. Transfer the chicken to a serving platter and set aside in a warm place.

Continue cooking the quinces for 5 minutes, until the pieces are soft but still holding their shape. Add to the platter, sprinkle the chives over all, and serve.

ABOUT BRINING

Presoaking poultry or other meats in a light salt brine was a technique more used when women, the designated home cooks, were at home rather than working outside the home during the day. It's not difficult to keep this step in our modern times with a little advance planning: Start the night before, or even on the morning of the day you are cooking the dish, by mixing together the salt solution, adding the chickens, and placing them in the refrigerator while you go about your business of the day. (Don't leave the meat in the brine longer than 24 hours, however, or it will become too salty.) The technique works also for seasoning and firming pork roast, rabbit, or trout.

Roasted Game Hens with Bread and Apricot Stuffing

🐦 Serves 4

Baking the stuffing both in and under the game hens results in a pleasing contrast between crisp and soft. The stuffing recipe can also be baked separately for a crunchy side dressing to accompany a Thanksgiving turkey (page 175).

Stuffing

> 4 tablespoons butter, melted
> 2 celery ribs, halved and thinly sliced
> ½ large yellow or white onion, finely chopped
> 12 dried apricot halves, coarsely chopped
> ½ cup coarsely chopped walnuts
> 4 cups fresh (½-inch) bread cubes, dry-toasted until
>   golden
> ¾ cup chopped fresh flat-leaf parsley
> 2 tablespoons dry sherry
> 1 teaspoon kosher salt
> ½ teaspoon freshly ground black pepper
>
> 2 game hens
> ¼ cup white wine

Preheat the oven to 425°F.

To make the stuffing, melt the butter in a large sauté pan over medium-high heat. Add the celery and onion and sauté until wilted, 5 minutes. Stir in the apricots and nuts and cook for 1 minute, until the apricots soften. Transfer to a large bowl, add the bread and remaining ingredients, and toss to mix. Set aside until completely cool.

Fill the cavity of each game hen with as much stuffing as will fit without packing it tightly. Spread the remaining stuffing on the bottom of a clay oven pot or roasting pan. Place the game hens on the stuffing bed and pour the wine over the top. Cover and roast for 40 minutes. Remove the cover and continue roasting until the hens are golden on top and the meat between the leg and thigh is no longer pink, 10 to 15 minutes. Serve right away.

Chicken and Wheat Porridge
Keshkeg, Herrisah

A humble dish that goes by two names, keshkeg and herrisah, is an ancient comfort food of chicken and wheat cooked and beaten together by hand to achieve a porridge consistency. To simplify the process while preserving its heritage, I offer a quicker and easier recipe that calls for cracked wheat rather than the traditional whole berries, because it takes less time to cook and uses an electric mixer for the beating. The seasoned butter topping can also be used as a finishing touch for many other dishes, for instance, grilled or sautéed chicken breasts or otherwise unadorned vegetables, such as zucchini, eggplant, or tomatoes.

1 cup bulgur, preferably coarse

3 cups boiling water

3 cups low-sodium chicken broth

4 boneless, skinless chicken thigh pieces, cut into
    1/4-inch-wide strips

1 teaspoon kosher salt

1/2 teaspoon freshly ground black pepper

8 large sprigs fresh flat-leaf parsley, with stems

Topping

4 tablespoons (1/2 stick) butter

1 teaspoon mild paprika

1 teaspoon ground cumin

1/4 teaspoon kosher salt

Place the bulgur in a bowl and pour the boiling water over it. Set aside to soak for 1 hour.

Drain the bulgur and transfer it to a large, heavy pot. Add the remaining ingredients and bring to a boil over high heat. Decrease the heat to maintain a gentle simmer and cook, covered, for 30 minutes, until the liquid is mostly absorbed. Remove the parsley and beat the mixture with an electric mixer until it is creamy and almost a puree, about 5 minutes.

In a small sauté pan, heat the butter with the paprika, cumin, and salt over medium heat until foaming. Pour over the porridge and serve.

VARIATIONS FOR KESHKEG

+ Instead of cumin, use cinnamon, curry powder, or allspice.
+ Accompany with a bowl of yogurt on the side.

All-American Armenian Thanksgiving Turkey with Wild Rice Pilaf and Cranberry Sauce

For Armenians, Saint's Day celebrations at church or just-the-family birthdays at home all provide welcome occasions to celebrate around food. For Armenians in America, Thanksgiving is always on the calendar to fill this need for convivial, food-centered gatherings. It is a gala affair, with turkey and all the trimmings. Here's my rendition of an Armenian-American Thanksgiving.

Serves 10 to 12

Cranberry Sauce

4 cups fresh cranberries, rinsed and picked over

¼ cup freshly squeezed tangerine juice

1 cup sugar

Turkey

1 (14- to 16-pound) turkey with giblets, giblets reserved

8 tablespoons (1 stick) butter, at room temperature

2 sprigs rosemary

4 sprigs thyme

Salt and freshly ground black pepper

❖

Recipe continues on next page

My dad with a rack and counter full of dressed turkeys for Thanksgiving in Japan, circa 1945.

Wild Rice Pilaf

> 6 tablespoons butter
> 1 cup walnut pieces
> ½ pound chanterelle or shiitake mushrooms, trimmed
>   and sliced ¼- to ½-inch thick
> 1 small yellow or white onion, finely chopped
> 1½ cups good-quality, hand-harvested wild rice
> 3 cups turkey broth (see box, page 178)
> ½ teaspoon chopped fresh thyme
> 1 teaspoon kosher salt
> ½ teaspoon Aleppo pepper
> 1 tablespoon chopped fresh flat-leaf parsley

To make the cranberry sauce, combine the cranberries, tangerine juice, and sugar in a heavy saucepan and bring to a boil over medium-high heat. Cook until the cranberries begin to pop, about 5 minutes. Stir to mix, decrease the heat to maintain a brisk simmer, and cook until thickened, 5 to

10 minutes, depending on the size of the pot. Remove from the heat and cool. Serve at room temperature or chilled. Will keep in the refrigerator for several months.

To cook the turkey, preheat the oven to 375°F.

Liberally salt and pepper the turkey inside and out. Place a double layer of cheesecloth over the breast and spread the butter over the cheesecloth. Place the rosemary and thyme sprigs over the butter and cover with another layer of cheesecloth. Place in the oven and roast for 15 minutes per pound, until an instant-read thermometer registers 162° in the thigh. For the last half hour, remove the cheesecloth so the breast can brown.

While the turkey cooks, make the pilaf. Melt 3 tablespoons of the butter in a large saucepan over medium-high heat. Add the walnuts and sauté until lightly toasted, 3 to 4 minutes. Transfer to a plate and set aside.

Add the mushrooms and onion to the same pan and sauté until the vegetables soften, about 5 minutes. Increase the heat to high, add the rice, and stir to mix and coat the grains. Add the broth, thyme, salt, and Aleppo pepper and bring to a boil. Decrease the heat to low, cover the pot, and cook until the rice is tender, about 40 minutes. Turn off the heat and set aside to steam-dry for 15 minutes. Stir in the walnuts and parsley and adjust the salt seasoning. Dot the top with the remaining 3 tablespoons butter and, without stirring, cover and set aside in a warm place until ready to serve.

To serve, transfer the turkey to a platter and carve. Accompany with the wild rice pilaf and the cranberry sauce in side dishes.

TURKEY BROTH FOR THANKSGIVING
WILD RICE PILAF

In keeping with the turkey theme of the day, use the giblets to make turkey broth for the pilaf. Place the neck, gizzard, and, if you care to, the wing tips from the turkey in a saucepan. Add ½ small yellow onion, 1 clove garlic, 1 small carrot, all coarsely cut up, along with 3 sprigs flat-leaf parsley and 4 cups water, and bring to a boil over high heat. Decrease the heat to maintain a brisk simmer and cook uncovered for 30 minutes, until reduced to about 3 cups. Strain through a fine mesh sieve set over a bowl and set aside at room temperature for up to 30 minutes, or store in the refrigerator for up to 3 days. Discard the solids from the strainer.

Grilled Duck with Walnut Pesto

I suggest Muscovy duck for its dark meat, reminiscent of the wild duck my Uncle Whitey might have bagged. The walnut pesto sauce, called taratour, is a classic of Armenian and Middle Eastern cuisine. It is also lavished on baked fish, fried mussels, fried eggplant, and boiled vegetables, such as green beans and cauliflower.

Serves 4

Duck

4 duck leg/thigh pieces
1 large clove garlic, finely chopped
2 tablespoons extra virgin olive oil
1 teaspoon chopped fresh thyme
½ teaspoon Aleppo pepper
½ teaspoon kosher salt

Walnut Pesto: Taratour

4 (1-inch-thick) slices baguette, crusts removed
    (stale bread is okay)
½ cup water
½ cup walnut pieces
1 clove garlic, minced or pressed
¼ teaspoon kosher salt
¼ cup extra virgin olive oil

Recipe continues on next page

2 teaspoons red wine vinegar

2 tablespoons water

Place the duck in a dish large enough to hold the pieces in one layer. Add the garlic, olive oil, thyme, Aleppo pepper, and salt and toss to mix and coat. Set aside to marinate at room temperature for 1 hour or refrigerate for up to 3 hours.

To make the taratour, place the bread and ½ cup water in a small bowl. Set aside to soak and soften for 5 minutes, then squeeze dry. Pulverize the walnuts in a food processor. Add the bread and remaining ingredients and puree. Set aside at room temperature until ready to use, up to 4 hours, or refrigerate for up to 3 days.

To cook the duck, prepare a medium-hot fire or preheat a gas grill to medium high. Grill the duck over indirect heat, turning 2 or 3 times, until medium to medium rare, 30 to 35 minutes.

Transfer to a platter and serve, accompanied with the taratour sauce on the side.

Grilled Quail Wrapped in Grape Leaves with Grape Kebabs

Grape leaves, used for wrapping sarmas (page 239) or stewed as a vegetable side dish (page 222), can also serve as an herby wrap for grilled meats, as they do here. The kebabs of whole grapes provide a sweet counterpoint to the leaves' tartness, and the whole rind of the lemon (including the white part) adds a definite lemon flavor with a touch of bitter.

Serves 4

> 1 lemon
> 2 tablespoons extra virgin olive oil
> 1 teaspoon kosher salt
> ½ teaspoon freshly ground black pepper
> 8 quail
> 16 large grape leaves, fresh or brined
> 24 plump green grapes, preferably Thompson seedless

To prepare the quail, peel the lemon using a vegetable peeler, cutting deeply enough to include some of the white part, and chop it. Place the chopped rind in a dish large enough to hold the quail side by side. Squeeze the juice out of the lemon and add it to the dish. Add the oil, salt, and pepper and stir to mix. Add the quail and turn to coat inside and out. Set aside in the refrigerator to marinate for 3 to 6 hours, but not longer or the delicate quail will become "pickled."

When ready to cook, prepare a medium-hot charcoal fire or preheat a gas grill to medium high.

Lift the quail out of the dish and, without wiping them off, wrap each one in grape leaves, using toothpicks to secure the leaves. String the grapes on 4 individual bamboo skewers (6 grapes per skewer).

Place the quail on the grill rack over indirect heat, cover the grill, and cook for 6 minutes. Turn and cook for 6 minutes more, until firm to the touch. Move the birds to directly over the fire and grill uncovered until the grape leaves are slightly charred and the quail is medium rare in the breast, about 2 minutes more. Transfer to a serving platter and let rest so that the juices settle while you cook the grape kebabs.

Place the kebabs on the grill directly over the heat and cook, turning once, until lightly charred and a little shriveled, about 6 minutes.

Add the grape kebabs to the platter with the quail and serve right away.

Aunt Rose's Roast Pheasant

Here's how my cousin Bob White, Aunt Rose's son, remembers his mother cooking the pheasant from his stepfather Whitey's coop, except for the wine, which Bob doesn't remember, and the allspice, which I've added for an extra Armenian touch. The lemon-juice rub, along with the orange juice and white wine in the basting sauce, add acid that tenderizes the pheasant meat.

Serves 2 to 3

1 young plump pheasant (about 2½ pounds)
Juice of ½ lemon
Kosher salt and freshly ground black pepper
2 tablespoons butter, at room temperature
½ cup raisins
⅓ cup freshly squeezed orange juice
1 teaspoon finely chopped lemon rind
⅛ teaspoon ground allspice
1 cup low-sodium chicken broth
⅓ cup white wine

Preheat the oven to 350°F.

Rub the pheasant inside and out with the lemon juice and a liberal amount of salt and pepper. Place in a baking dish breast side up and spread the butter over the breast and legs.

In a bowl, mix together the raisins, orange juice, lemon rind, allspice, broth, and wine. Pour over the pheasant and bake, basting every 10 minutes, for 50 minutes, until the meat is no longer pink between the breast and wing meat.

Remove from the oven and transfer the pheasant to a platter. Set aside in a warm place. Pour the pan juices into a small saucepan, bring to a boil over high heat, and cook until thickened and saucy and reduced by half, about 7 minutes.

Pour the sauce over the pheasant and serve, carving at the table.

Aunt Rose, my father's sister, and her son, cousin Bob White, dressed up for Sunday. Not sure if Bob likes his outfit, but he looks cute!

Rabbit Fricassee with Dried Figs and Boiling Onions

Rather than accompanying the rabbit, the liver and kidneys can be cooked in advance and served with baguette slices as a "kitchen" maza, to enjoy while diners await the fricassee.

Serves 4 to 6

4 tablespoons (½ stick) butter

1 tablespoon extra virgin olive oil

Kosher salt

1 (2½-pound) rabbit, cut into 6 serving pieces and brined
    (optional, see page 169), liver and kidneys reserved
    separately

¼ teaspoon ground cloves

½ teaspoon ground coriander

⅛ teaspoon cinnamon

¼ teaspoon freshly ground black pepper

1 cup white wine

2 tablespoons freshly squeezed lemon juice

1 cup water

6 Calimyrna or Kalamata golden dried figs, quartered

6 small boiling onions, peeled

1 teaspoon chopped fresh flat-leaf parsley, for garnish

1 teaspoon chopped fresh mint, for garnish

Melt 2 tablespoons of the butter with the olive oil in a large sauté pan over medium-high heat.

Pat the rabbit pieces dry, sprinkle with salt, and add them to the pan.

Poultry, Game, and Eggs · 185

Cook, turning once, to brown on both sides, about 5 minutes. (Work in batches if necessary to keep from crowding the pan.)

Add the cloves, coriander, cinnamon, pepper, wine, lemon juice, and water, and stir to mix. Bring to a boil, decrease the heat to maintain a simmer, cover, and cook for 1 hour.

Add the figs and onions, cover again, and simmer for 30 minutes more, until the rabbit is tender. Remove from the heat and let rest 10 minutes for the juices to settle.

In a small sauté pan, melt the remaining 2 tablespoons butter over medium heat until foaming. Add the liver and kidneys and sprinkle with salt and pepper. Sauté until firm but still pink in the centers, about 6 minutes. Remove from the heat and set aside in a warm place.

To serve, arrange the rabbit, figs, and onions on a serving platter and pour the pan juices over the top. Slice the liver and kidneys, place them on a separate small plate, and sprinkle the parsley over the top. Sprinkle the mint over the rabbit and serve.

Cousin Gary's Rabbit Pie with Onion Confit, Pancetta, Mushrooms, and Sage

Serves 4 to 6

When we were kids, my cousin Gary Jenanyan, chef extraordinaire, lived around the block from my grandmother's and aunt's houses in Sacramento. We often shared in food celebrations—he always won the Easter egg cracking game (page 195)—and we still do. He calls this stellar dish somewhat un-Armenian, but then, Armenians do love onions, mushrooms, and good food of any style. Making the onion confit by first wilting the onion in water before caramelizing is a professional tip to treasure: The confit comes out sweet as can be, and low fat. Gary includes the rabbit liver only if it is buttery fresh. For a simpler dish, the rabbit and onion confit can be combined and served over pasta. In place of the hard-to-find chervil sprigs, a mix of 1 teaspoon chopped fresh tarragon and 1 tablespoon fresh flat-leaf parsley can be substituted.

4 thin slices pancetta (Italian unsmoked bacon), cut
    crosswise into 1-inch pieces

1 (2¼- to 2½-pound) rabbit, with kidneys and liver,
    rabbit cut into 6 pieces

3 tablespoons butter

2 ounces fresh chanterelle or shiitake mushrooms,
    trimmed and sliced ¼ inch thick

1 clove garlic, minced or pressed

1 teaspoon chopped fresh sage leaves

Kosher salt and freshly ground black pepper

½ medium yellow or white onion, coarsely chopped

1 clove garlic, coarsely chopped

1 small carrot, coarsely chopped

¼ cup white wine

1½ cups low-sodium chicken broth

Onion Confit

1 large yellow or white onion, halved and thinly
sliced

⅓ cup water

2 tablespoons butter

2 tablespoons butter, melted

8 (12 × 13-inch) sheets fillo

12 sprigs fresh chervil, for garnishing, or 1 teaspoon
chopped fresh tarragon and 1 tablespoon chopped
fresh flat-leaf parsley

Place the pancetta in a large, heavy sauté pan over medium-high heat, and sauté until wilted, 3 to 5 minutes. Add the rabbit kidneys and liver, if using, and cook, stirring often, until the pancetta is browned and the kidneys are firm to the touch, about 4 minutes. With a slotted spoon, transfer the pancetta, kidneys, and liver to a large bowl, leaving the fat in the pan, and set aside. When cool enough to handle, coarsely chop the kidneys and return to the bowl.

Add 2 tablespoons of the butter to the same pan and let it melt over medium heat. Add the mushrooms, minced garlic, and sage and sauté until the mushrooms are well wilted, about 5 minutes. Transfer to the bowl with the pancetta and kidneys and set aside.

To cook the rabbit, melt the remaining 1 tablespoon of butter in the same pan. Season the rabbit pieces with salt and pepper. Working in batches, add as many pieces as will fit without crowding and brown them on both sides, 5 to 6 minutes. Transfer the pieces to a plate. When all the rabbit is browned, add the chopped onion, chopped garlic, carrot, wine, and broth to the pan. Bring to a boil over high heat, cover, and simmer for 15 minutes. Turn over the rabbit pieces and continue cooking, covered, until tender enough to pull off the bones with a fork, about 25 minutes. Remove from the heat and let cool in the broth for 15 minutes.

My dad's cousin, Armen Jenanyan, with his wife, Helen Jenanyan, and their children (my cousins) Gary and Karen.

With a slotted spoon, lift the rabbit out of the broth. With your fingers and a paring knife, remove the rabbit meat from the bones. Discard the bones. Cut the meat into bite-size pieces and add to the bowl with the mushrooms and other ingredients. Strain the liquid into a small saucepan. Bring to a boil over medium-high heat and cook until reduced to about 1 cup, 10 to 15 minutes, depending on the size of the saucepan. Set aside.

While the rabbit cooks and cools, make the onion confit. Place the onions and water in a large, heavy sauté pan and bring to a boil over medium-high heat. Decrease the heat to medium and cook uncovered until the onions are well wilted and the liquid is mostly evaporated, about 8 minutes. Add the butter and cook until the onions are golden and lightly caramelized, about 8 minutes. Set aside.

To assemble and cook the pie, preheat the oven to 375°F. Lightly grease a 9 × 12-inch baking dish with a little of the melted butter.

Lay 2 fillo sheets in the bottom of the pie dish and brush with butter. Add 2 more sheets, brush with butter, then 2 more sheets and brush with butter. Spread the rabbit mixture over the fillo, then spread the onion confit over the rabbit. Pour in the reduced juices and cover the pie with 6 more layers of fillo, buttering every second sheet as above. Place in the oven and bake until golden and crispy, about 35 minutes.

Cut into serving portions, garnish each with chervil sprigs, and serve hot.

Armenian Omelette with Tomato and Chive

Serves 2 to 3

Armenians love omelettes as much as the Greeks or French do, especially Caucasian Armenians, who make a wide variety based on various vegetables rather than cheese for extra flavor. The omelettes, and other egg dishes (see the following two recipes), are served around the clock, for breakfast, light meals, or snacks on the maza table.

> 2 tablespoons butter
> 1 medium tomato, peeled, seeded, and finely chopped
> 2 tablespoons finely chopped green bell pepper
> ¼ teaspoon ground cumin
> 1 tablespoon chopped fresh chives
> ½ teaspoon kosher salt
> ¼ teaspoon Aleppo pepper
> 4 large eggs, lightly beaten

Melt the butter in a medium sauté pan over medium-high heat. Add the tomato, bell pepper, cumin, chive, salt, and Aleppo pepper and stir to mix. Cook until no longer moist, about 2 minutes. Stir in the eggs and cook until they begin to set and form a solid base, 2 to 3 minutes. With a spatula, flip one half over to make a half-moon shape and continue cooking for 1 minute more, until set but still moist inside. Transfer to a platter and serve right away.

OMELETTE CUM FRITTATA

As often as not, omelettes are made frittata-style—baked in the oven rather than cooked on the stove top. To make a baked omelet, preheat the oven to 350°F. Using a pan with an ovenproof handle, follow the recipe to the point of adding the eggs. Rather than cook on the stove top, place the pan in the oven and cook until the eggs set, 15 to 20 minutes. Slice and serve.

Oven-Poached Eggs on a Bed of Spinach and Yogurt

Cooking the eggs in small ramekins makes for cute, individual servings, but you can also cook them side by side in a single glass baking dish. The timing is the same.

Serves 4

1 bunch (about ¾ pound) spinach
2 tablespoons butter
½ small yellow or white onion, finely chopped
2 tablespoons yogurt
1 teaspoon chopped fresh dill
½ teaspoon kosher salt
4 large eggs
Salt and freshly ground black pepper, to taste

To prepare the spinach, cut off the stems, wash the leaves well, drain, and transfer to a heavy pot or microwave bowl. Cover and cook over high heat on the stove top or on high in the microwave just until the leaves are wilted but still bright green, 3 to 5 minutes either way. Drain and cool enough to handle. Squeeze out excess water, chop finely, and set aside.

Preheat the oven to 375°F. In a sauté pan, melt the butter over medium-high heat. Add the onion and cook for 2 minutes, until slightly wilted. Add the spinach, yogurt, dill, and ½ teaspoon salt and stir to mix. Cook for 1 minute more, until the moisture is mostly gone.

Divide the spinach mixture among four 1-cup ramekins. Break an egg into each ramekin. Place in the oven and bake until the white is set and the yolk is done as you like, about 15 minutes. Sprinkle with salt and freshly ground black pepper and serve right away.

Fried Eggs with Mock Basterma

Fried eggs coupled with basterma is an Armenian speciality, and a perfect dish for an all-American Sunday brunch, along with Choeregs (page 60), perhaps some Green Fig and Fennel Seed Marmalade (page 61), coffee, and a pitcher of freshly squeezed orange juice. If you don't have the mock basterma, prosciutto can substitute nicely.

2 tablespoons butter
12 thin slices Mock
     Basterma (page 43)
4 large eggs
Kosher salt and freshly
     ground black pepper,
     to taste

Serves 4

"Uncle" Doc Jenanyan, Hatcher's brother, and Uncle Doc's wife, Grandma Rose, with my cousins Gary and Karen, 1951.

Melt the butter in a medium sauté pan over medium heat. Arrange the basterma slices in an overlapping layer in the pan and cook for 30 seconds, until the basterma begins to shrink. Crack the eggs into the pan over the basterma and cook until the eggs set, 3 to 5 minutes, depending on how well done you like them. Serve right away, accompanied with the dishes suggested above, if using.

EASTER EGGS

One day my cousin Gary Jenanyan and I were reminiscing about our shared memories of Easter, a big Armenian holiday we sometimes spent together in Sacramento with all the relatives. He eloquently described the lively, fun-for-kids part of the day:

"By the time our Easter baskets were full, we were ready to wrestle and foist and raise mischief any way we could. The adults had designed a ritual exactly to suit this purpose, and it was a highlight of the Easter get-togethers. The game was to keep your own egg intact while smashing all the others. You tightly hold an egg in the fist, exposing as little as possible of its end through a nickel-sized, open circle formed by your thumb and forefinger. The game plan was to reveal as little surface as possible through a tiny hand—you had to show some—so as not to expose too much to the bang of the other. Total triumph was to stand holding the last uncracked egg."

We can't remember how much egg salad turned up from all the cracked eggs, or how long the winner's egg sat as trophy on the shelf before being discreetly plopped into the garbage. We do remember that it was always a marvelously boisterous round of indulging the children, and we now do the same with our own kids. Here's our recipe for not-too-bouncy, tender hard-boiled eggs.

FOR 3 DOZEN EGGS

> 36 large white eggs
> Water

Place the eggs in a pot large enough to hold them in 2 layers (you may need to use 2 pots). Add water to cover and bring to a boil over medium-high heat. Cover the pot, remove it from the heat, and let sit for 13 minutes.

Ever so gently, drain off the water, then run cold water into the pan until the eggs are cool enough to handle. Use to dye for an Easter egg hunt, or peel them and enjoy as deviled eggs or egg salad.

Fish and Seafood

❖

From maza to entrée, Armenian tables sport piscene dishes: freshwater fish of many kinds from local inland rivers and lakes and saltwater offerings from the nearby Caspian, Black, Aegean, and Mediterranean seas. I love seafood and serve it often. This chapter contains nine fish dishes I call Armenian cooking in twenty-first-century style.

Grilled Trout

The waters of the Caucasus Mountains are famous for the excellence of their trout. Lake Sevan in northeastern Armenia, one of the world's largest and highest mountain lakes, especially boasts a reputation of serving up incomparable trout to vacationers, who enjoy the fish in the restaurants and cafés on the lake's banks within minutes of its being caught. I understand the romance of catching and cooking trout on the spot: Trout fishing expeditions in the Rocky Mountains of Colorado and New Mexico were regular family vacations when I was growing up. We pangrilled the catch in a cast-iron skillet over a fire built on a gravelly riverbank ten feet from where we had just reeled it in. Pristinely fresh, it was utterly delicious with merely a light seasoning and a simple garnish of lemon wedges and parsley, and that's how I still prepare trout. If you prefer a little more saucing, accompany the fish with Lemon, Cilantro, and Scallion Sauce (page 200). To ensure freshness, purchase head-on trout with very clear eyes and glistening skin.

Serves 2

> 2 (10- to 12-ounce) or 1 (1¼ pound) fresh, bone-in
>   whole trout
> 2 tablespoons freshly squeezed lemon juice
> Kosher salt and Aleppo pepper
> 2 tablespoons chopped fresh flat-leaf parsley
> 1 lemon, cut into 4 wedges

Prepare a medium-hot charcoal fire or preheat a gas grill to medium high. Rinse the trout, pat them dry, and season them inside and out with the lemon juice and a light sprinkling of salt and Aleppo pepper. Set aside at room temperature until the fire is ready. To cook, grill the trout directly

over the heat, turning once, until no longer pink along the backbone, 8 to 9 minutes for small trout, 10 to 12 minutes for large trout.

Transfer the trout to a platter. With your fingers, gently remove and discard the skin. Sprinkle the trout with the parsley, garnish the platter with the lemon wedges, and serve right away.

Grilled Mackerel with Lemon, Cilantro, and Scallion Sauce

Mackerel, with its gamy flavor, requires a punchy sauce, such as this one, which is also popular for garnishing trout or other grilled fish.

Serves 4

2 (10- to 12-ounce) mackerel
Kosher salt and freshly ground black pepper
2 tablespoons freshly squeezed lemon juice

Sauce

¼ cup freshly squeezed lemon juice
¼ cup extra virgin olive oil
2 tablespoons chopped cilantro
2 tablespoons finely chopped scallions
½ teaspoon kosher salt
¼ teaspoon freshly ground black pepper

Prepare a medium-hot charcoal fire or preheat a gas grill to medium high. Season the mackerel inside and out with salt, pepper, and the lemon juice and set aside at room temperature until the fire is ready.

To make the sauce, stir together all the ingredients in a small bowl. Set aside.

To cook, grill the mackerel directly over the heat, turning once, until the flesh is flaky and no longer pink at the backbone, 13 to 15 minutes. Serve right away, with the sauce on the side.

Arayah Jenanyan's Grilled Salmon Fillets Wrapped in Fig Leaves

*Serves 4

My sister, Arayah Jenanyan, created this dish one day as she was admiring the fig tree in her Berkeley, California, garden. With local Pacific salmon in season, she put the fig leaves and fish together in an inspired way. Fig leaves impart a fresh cinnamony taste, a favorite Armenian seasoning, that goes particularly well with salmon, sardines, or quail. If you don't have access to fresh fig leaves, grape leaves can substitute.

> 4 to 8 fresh fig leaves, depending on the size, rinsed
>   and patted dry
> Extra virgin olive oil, for brushing on the leaves
> 4 (6-ounce) salmon fillets
> 1 large shallot, thinly sliced
> Kosher salt and freshly ground black pepper
> Lemon wedges or Lemon, Cilantro, and Scallion Sauce
>   (page 200), for serving

Prepare a medium-low charcoal fire or preheat a gas grill to medium low.

Lightly brush the fig leaves on both sides with olive oil (to make them more supple and keep them from sticking to the grill). Place the salmon fillets on the rough sides of the fig leaves. Spread shallot slices over the fillets and sprinkle with salt and pepper. Fold over the leaves to enclose the fillets and make a packet. (Use a second leaf if necessary to wrap the fillets entirely.) Secure the packets with toothpicks and set aside at room temperature until the fire is ready.

To cook, place the packets directly over the heat and grill until the fish is firm to the touch and the leaves are slightly charred, 9 to 10 minutes. Transfer to a platter or individual plates and serve right away, accompanied with the lemon wedges or sauce on the side. (The diners unwrap the packet themselves, discarding the leaves.

Fried Fish Marinated in Orange, Lemon, and Garlic

A delicious and very simple Armenian way to prepare white-fish fillets is to marinate them briefly in citrus and fry them quickly on the stove top.

Serves 4

⅓ cup freshly squeezed orange juice

2 tablespoons freshly squeezed lemon juice

1 large clove garlic, minced or pressed

½ teaspoon kosher salt

½ teaspoon Aleppo pepper

1½ pounds white-fish fillets (½ inch thick), such as
   red snapper or petrale sole

2 tablespoons extra virgin olive oil, for frying

All-purpose flour, for dusting the fish

2 tablespoons chopped fresh flat-leaf parsley, mint,
   dill, or cilantro, for garnish

In a dish large enough to hold the fish in one layer, stir together the orange juice, lemon juice, garlic, salt, and pepper. Add the fish, turn to coat, and set aside to marinate for 30 minutes at room temperature. (Do not let them marinate longer than 30 to 40 minutes, or they will become "pickled.")

To cook the fish, lift the fillets out of the marinade, pat them dry, and dust lightly with flour on both sides. Heat the oil in a large sauté pan over medium-high heat. Add the fillets, without crowding, and fry, turning once, until flaky and golden on both sides, 5 to 6 minutes. Sprinkle the herb you are using over the top and serve right away.

Fish Baked in Parchment with Butter, Garlic, Herbs, and Capers

In the Eastern Mediterranean, this "fancy" fish dish is seasoned with dill; in Cau-casian Armenia, cooks are more inclined to use tarragon for the herb. On the coast of California, where I live, I choose either dill or tarragon, according to which looks fresh and lively in my garden or the market that day. Parchment paper, widely available in supermarkets, is the wrap of choice. Waxed paper or aluminum foil also work, though neither looks as refined when you present the dish.

Serves 4

Butter, for greasing the baking sheet
1½ pounds thick white-fish fillets, such as halibut,
     cod, snapper, orange roughy, or petrale sole, cut
     into four 6-ounce portions
8 very thin lemon slices
4 tablespoons butter
2 large cloves garlic, pressed
1 rounded tablespoon capers, rinsed and drained
1 tablespoon chopped fresh flat-leaf parsley
1 teaspoon chopped fresh dill or tarragon
4 to 8 (depending on the size) thin slices ripe tomato
Kosher salt
Freshly ground black pepper
¼ cup white wine

Preheat the oven to 375°F. Lightly butter a baking sheet large enough to hold the packets without overlapping.

Cut four 13 × 15-inch rectangles of parchment paper and lay them out on a counter. Place a fish fillet in the center of each and sprinkle with salt. Place 2 lemon slices and one-quarter of the butter on each fillet. Sprinkle each fillet with one-quarter of the garlic, capers, parsley, and dill or tarragon. Top with the tomato slices, cutting them in half if they are large, a sprinkling of salt and pepper, and finally a splash of the wine. Fold up the parchment to make an envelope package and set the packages on the baking sheet seam side down.

Bake for 18 to 20 minutes, until the fish is flaky and the juices bubbly (see box). Transfer the packets to individual plates and serve right away, allowing each diner to unfold the packet *à table*.

WHEN IS THE FISH DONE?

Judging the doneness of the fish when it's wrapped in parchment, out of sight, can be tricky. Experienced cooks tell by pressing gently through the parchment and gauging its "spring back." It should be firm, but not bouncy. Another way is to carefully unwrap a package, taking care to avoid the escaping steam, and see if the fish has reached the right flaky-but-still-juicy stage.

White Fish Plaki-Style with Lemon and Curry

Serves 4

Plaki-style is the description for oven or stove-top braising of fish with vegetables, such as leeks or onions, carrot, celery, and often potatoes, in an aromatic tomato broth, or sometimes the plaki is just of vegetables alone. It's a preparation familiar in daily fare throughout the Eastern Mediterranean and all the way north to Armenian kitchens in the Caucasus. Though I have never seen curry included in an Armenian plaki dish, I find its addition makes the dish special, but still easy. You can omit the potatoes and serve the plaki with one of the rice pilafs (pages 250–256) instead.

1¼ pounds white-fish fillets, such as sea bass, halibut,
   or snapper
3 tablespoons freshly squeezed lemon juice
1½ teaspoons kosher salt
4 small Yukon gold potatoes, sliced 1 inch thick
¼ cup extra virgin olive oil
1 leek, thinly sliced
2 ribs celery, thinly sliced
2 medium ripe tomatoes, coarsely chopped
½ cup white wine or water
2 teaspoons curry powder
½ teaspoon Aleppo pepper
2 tablespoons chopped fresh flat-leaf parsley, for garnish

Preheat the oven to 350°F. Bring a large pot of water to boil.

Place the fish fillets in one layer in a large baking dish and sprinkle on both sides with half of the lemon juice and salt. Set aside at room temperature for 15 to 30 minutes while preparing the vegetables.

Place the potatoes in the boiling water and cook until half tender, about 5 minutes. Drain and set aside.

In a large sauté pan, heat the oil over medium-high heat. Add the leek and celery and sauté until limp, about 3 minutes. Stir in the tomato, wine or water, curry powder, Aleppo pepper, and remaining lemon juice and salt. Continue cooking until the tomato softens, about 3 minutes.

Tuck the potatoes under the fish in the baking dish. Pour the vegetables and sauce from the sauté pan over the top. Bake for 30 to 40 minutes, depending on the kind and thickness of the fillets, until cooked through and beginning to flake. Remove from the oven and let rest for 5 minutes.

Sprinkle the parsley over the top and serve right away.

Red Snapper Stew with
Baby Artichokes and Potatoes

Red snapper, though pleasingly textured, can be bland. But combined with arti-chokes and potatoes in a plaki-style preparation cooked on the stove top, its draw-backs are minimized while its advantages are accented in an out-of-the-ordinary, yet very Armenian, delicious fish stew.

Note: If you cannot find baby artichokes, use canned or frozen artichoke hearts.

Serves 4

12 (about 1 pound) baby artichokes

6 (about ½ pound) fingerling or creamer potatoes,
    scrubbed and cut in half

1½ pounds red snapper fillets (½ to ¾ inch thick)

1 teaspoon kosher salt

2 tablespoons extra-virgin olive oil

1½ cups low-sodium chicken broth

1 large clove garlic, minced or pressed

2 teaspoons freshly squeezed lemon juice

1 tablespoon chopped fresh flat-leaf parsley or cilantro,
    for garnish

To prepare the artichokes, bring a pot of salted water to boil over high heat. Cut the stems off the artichokes, pull off the tough outer leaves, and cut the tops off down to the light green part of the leaves. Drop into the boiling water and cook until tender, about 10 minutes. With a wire strainer, transfer the artichokes to a colander and set aside to drain. When cool enough to handle, cut them in half.

In the same water, cook the potatoes until tender, 10 to 12 minutes, depending on the size. Drain and set aside.

Heat the oil in a large sauté pan over medium-high heat. Sprinkle the fish fillets liberally with salt and add them, without crowding, to the pan. Sauté, turning once, until flaky and cooked through, about 6 minutes. Transfer the fillets to a serving platter and set aside in a warm place.

Add the chicken broth, garlic, artichokes, and potatoes to the pan and bring to a boil over high heat. Cook until the liquid is reduced by half, 3 to 5 minutes. Stir in the lemon juice and parsley and continue cooking for 1 to 2 minutes more, until the liquid is thickened and saucy.

To serve, arrange the artichokes and potatoes around the fish. Spoon the sauce over the fish and vegetables, sprinkle the parsley over all, and serve right away.

Mussels in Tomato Onion Broth
with Toasted Breadcrumb Topping

Fresh mussels are a regularly available treat for families in many parts of the world,
and one I have long enjoyed, from plucking them myself off ocean rocks at low tide
to buying them from the fish counter, still alive, imported from Prince Edward Is-
land or even New Zealand. It must be an atavistic taste because when preparing
this book, I turned back east to my ancestral home in what is now Turkey and dis-
covered favored Armenian recipes for them. Following are two, one modern, the
other an Old World specialty (page 212). This is the modern Armenian preparation.

Serves 2 to 3

Toasted Breadcrumb Topping

 2 tablespoons butter
 ½ baguette or 2 slices country-style bread
   (1 inch thick), crust cut off, bread coarsely chopped

Mussels

 3 ripe tomatoes, coarsely chopped
 1 small yellow or white onion, halved and thinly sliced
 ½ cup white wine
 ½ cup water
 ¼ teaspoon kosher salt

2 pounds prepared mussels (see box, below),
    debearded if necessary
2 tablespoons chopped fresh flat-leaf parsley

To make the topping, melt the butter over medium heat until foaming. Add the bread and cook, stirring, until toasted, 3 to 4 minutes. Set aside.

Combine the tomato, onion, wine, water, and salt in a large, heavy pot and bring to a boil over high heat. Decrease the heat to maintain a simmer and cook for 10 minutes, until the tomatoes and onions have collapsed and the broth is no longer raw-tasting. Add the mussels, increase the heat to high, cover, and cook until the mussels open and are just firm, 4 to 6 minutes.

To serve, ladle the mussels and juices into individual bowls, discarding any mussels that haven't opened. Sprinkle the breadcrumb topping and parsley over the top, and serve right away.

PREPARING MUSSELS FOR THE POT

To make sure the mussels are fresh and lively, place them in a large bowl and fill it with cold water. Wait a minute and then squeeze each mussel to see if it closes. Transfer the ones that close to the "good" pile and discard those that don't close up. This way, you ensure that the duds won't taint the dish.

Stuffed Mussels
Midia Dolma

In a reverse take on paella, Armenians prepare the rice with its flavorings and stuff it inside the mussels rather than set the mussels on top of the rice. It's a traditional favorite, and a special dish for grand parties, usually served cold as an appetizer on the maza table. I find it worthy of star status on its own for an entrée and like to serve it hot. I cook the rice mixture first, with an untraditional addition of fresh fennel and a pinch of saffron. Then I steam the mussels open so they can easily be filled without fussing to pry them open with a knife while they are raw. Finally, I briefly reheat the midia dolmas just before serving. Any leftover stuffing may be served cold or warm as a side dish.

Makes 36 midia dolmas, serves 12 as a maza or 6 as an entrée

Stuffing

2 tablespoons extra virgin olive oil

1 cup finely chopped yellow or white onion

¼ cup finely chopped fresh fennel bulb

⅓ cup long grain white rice

⅓ cup finely chopped tomato, fresh or canned

1 tablespoon currants

1½ tablespoons pine nuts

Small pinch of cinnamon

Large pinch of saffron threads

½ teaspoon kosher salt

¼ teaspoon Aleppo pepper

¾ cup water

Mussels

>   36 prepared mussels (see page 211)
>   ½ cup water
>   ¼ cup chopped fresh flat-leaf parsley, for garnish
>   Lemon wedges, for garnish

To prepare the stuffing, heat the oil in a saucepan over medium-high heat. Add the onion and fennel and sauté for 3 minutes, until the vegetables wilt. Stir in the rice and sauté for 3 minutes, until the rice is translucent. Add the remaining ingredients and bring to a boil. Cover, decrease the heat to low, and cook for 25 minutes, until the rice is done. Set aside to steam dry and cool for 10 minutes, or up to several hours.

To prepare the mussels, place them in a large, heavy pot with the water. Cover the pot and cook for 5 minutes on high heat, until the mussels open. Remove and let cool enough to handle. Discard any mussels that haven't opened.

To assemble the dolmas, break apart the shell halves of each mussel. Pull off the beards and sever each mussel from the half shell it is attached to, leaving the mussel in the shell. (Discard the other half shells.) Mound 1½ to 2 tablespoons of the stuffing on top of each mussel.

Serve the mussels chilled, or reheat briefly in the microwave or a hot oven. Either way, sprinkle with the parsley, garnish with the lemon wedges, and serve.

STUFFED MUSSELS THE EASY WAY OUT: UNSTUFFED, AS PAELLA

The mussels can also be served paella-style: While the stuffing is hot, spread it on an oven- or microwave-safe serving dish. Top with the mussels in their half-shells and reheat briefly, about 2 minutes. Garnish with the parsley and lemon wedges as above and serve hot.

Vegetables: Roasted, Stewed, Stuffed

❖

Since the beginning of agriculture, Armenians have farmed their fertile lands, which supplied grains and vegetables aplenty for their tables. As a result, vegetables take a prominent place in Armenian cuisine. Sometimes they are prepared with simple additions; sometimes they are more complex, as in the many beloved stuffed vegetable compositions. Certainly, they are never just boiled. This chapter offers a menu of treasured Armenian vegetable preparations, plus some from the coastal California perspective of my American-Armenian upbringing.

Fried Eggplant

Fried eggplant slices are routinely accompanied with Taratour Sauce (page 179), but I prefer them with a simple sprinkling of lemon juice or, as my mother served them, in a sandwich (see box, page 217). It's important to pre-salt and wilt the slices because that way they quickly fry up golden without absorbing too much oil.

Makes about 20 slices, serves 10 to 12 as maza, 6 for a vegetable side dish or sandwich filling

> 1 large (1- to 1¼-pound) eggplant
> 2 teaspoons kosher salt
> Extra virgin olive oil, for frying
> 2 tablespoons freshly squeezed lemon juice,
>   for serving

Cut off the stem end of the eggplant and slice it into ¼-inch-thick rounds. Sprinkle the salt on both sides of each round and arrange them side by side on a layer of paper towels. Cover with another layer of paper towels and set aside to weep and wilt for 30 minutes.

To cook the eggplant, heat ⅛ inch of olive oil in a large, nonstick skillet over medium-high heat until sizzling. Pat the eggplant slices dry. Place as many slices as will fit without crowding in the skillet and fry, turning once, until golden on both sides, 6 to 8 minutes. Transfer to paper towels to drain and continue with another batch until all the slices are fried.

To serve, arrange the slices on a platter. Sprinkle with the lemon juice and serve at room temperature or chilled.

MY MOTHER'S EGGPLANT SANDWICHES

These were a frequent Saturday lunch treat for the family. Upon reflection, I think they must have been one of the strong influences on my love for fusion food at its best: Eschewing any batter, as I still do, though it's more traditional, my mother fried the eggplant and served them as a sandwich filling between bread slices spread with mayonnaise! That was her "battering," sliced bread instead of flour or breadcrumbs, and mayonnaise for sauce instead of taratour or lemon. What a delicious meeting of Armenia, California, and the American Southwest, all in a simple sandwich. In those days, the bread was American pre-sliced white bread. Now, I choose a tastier artisan bread, such as pain de mie, pain au levain, or a rustic Italian loaf, and, as a latter-day innovation, I add a lettuce leaf to each sandwich.

To make eggplant sandwiches:

Prepare and fry the eggplant as above. Spread one side of twelve ½-inch-thick slices of country-style bread with mayonnaise. Arrange 3 to 4 overlapping slices of eggplant over six of the bread slices on the mayonnaise side. Top with a romaine or butter lettuce leaf. Cover each with one of the 6 remaining bread slices, mayonnaise side down, to make a sandwich. Serve right away.

Grilled Eggplant

Whenever he was grilling our dinner, whether shish kebab, lamb chops, hamburgers, or chicken, my father, the grill chef, always tossed a whole eggplant directly into the coals while the fire was still very hot to charbroil it, and we would have grilled eggplant for a side dish. It was served plain, seasoned only with salt and pepper; he wasn't an ardent lover of garlic. But I am, and I always press a clove across the pulp before serving. Butter, rather than olive oil, is essential here.

Note: You can also cook the eggplant in an oven at 400°F for the same amount of time.

🐦 Serves 3 to 4

My dad, on the left, in chef's toque with a coworker, circa 1945.

1 large (1- to 1¼-pound) eggplant
2 tablespoons butter
1 large clove garlic, minced or pressed
Kosher salt and freshly ground black pepper

Prepare a hot charcoal fire or preheat a gas grill to high. Place the eggplant in the coals of the fire or directly over the heat on a gas grill. Cook, turning once or twice, until collapsed and charred all around, 40 to 50 minutes, depending on the size. Transfer to a serving plate and let rest for 5 to 10 minutes.

Slit the eggplant open lengthwise. Dot the butter and garlic over the pulp, sprinkle with salt and pepper, and serve.

Artichokes Braised in Olive Oil with Leek, Shallot, and Dill

Stewing artichokes with onion is a classic Armenian preparation. Traditionally, it is served chilled, but I also like it warm, especially when it's a vegetable accompaniment. Either way, the artichokes, being high in potassium, calcium, phosphorous, and fiber, make a healthful, delicious, low-calorie maza or side dish.

Serves 8

⅓ cup extra virgin olive oil

¼ cup freshly squeezed lemon juice

2 cups water

1 teaspoon sugar

½ teaspoon Aleppo pepper

4 medium artichokes, stems, tough outer leaves, and
    thorny tops cut off

8 small shallots, peeled and left whole

1 leek, white and light green part, slivered lengthwise

1 tablespoon chopped fresh dill

1 teaspoon kosher salt

Combine the oil, lemon juice, water, sugar, and Aleppo pepper in a heavy pot large enough to hold the artichokes in one packed layer. Cut the artichokes in half lengthwise. With a grapefruit spoon or paring knife, remove the chokes. Place the artichokes cut sides down in the pot, then turn cut sides up. Place a shallot in the center of each half. Spread the leeks over the top and sprinkle with the dill and salt. Cover and bring to a boil over medium-high heat. Decrease the heat to maintain a brisk simmer and cook for 25 minutes, until the shallots are soft and the artichokes are tender.

With a slotted spoon, transfer the artichokes and shallots to a platter. Increase the heat to high and reduce the liquid in the pot until thickened, about 5 minutes. Spoon over the artichokes and serve right away.

Grape Leaves Stewed with Tomato and Lemon

In late summer, when the grape leaves on the vine are large and no longer tender enough for sarma and the tomatoes on their own vines are juicy ripe, you can put them to delicious use together in this multi-purpose Armenian vegetable dish. Serve it as a topping for any of the bulgur pilafs (pages 259–261), as a condiment alongside kuftas or simple fried white fish (page 203), or as a filling in boerek (page 77). You can also use jarred grape leaves; rinse them well.

Makes about 3 cups

8 packed cups fresh grape leaves, or 1 (24-ounce)
    jar brined grape leaves, stems cut off
1 large tomato, peeled, seeded, and coarsely chopped
¼ cup freshly squeezed lemon juice
½ teaspoon Aleppo pepper
2 cups water

Cut the grape leaves into 1-inch-wide shreds and place them in a large nonreactive pot. Add the remaining ingredients, stir to mix, and bring to a boil over medium-high heat. Cover and cook for 15 minutes, until the leaves are completely wilted and beginning to soften. Remove the cover, decrease the heat to maintain a simmer, and continue cooking for 10 minutes, until the leaves are tender. Serve warm or cold. Will keep in the refrigerator for up to 2 weeks.

Roasted Beets in Yogurt Dill Sauce

Roasting the beets brings out their earthy, candylike flavor, which is accentuated by the balsamic vinegar.

Serves 4

12 baby beets or 4 medium beets, tops trimmed off
    and reserved for another dish
1 tablespoon extra virgin olive oil
Kosher salt and freshly ground black pepper
1 tablespoon balsamic vinegar
½ cup yogurt, stirred to smooth
¼ cup chopped fresh dill

Preheat the oven to 375°F.

If using baby beets, leave them whole; if using medium-size beets, cut them in half. Place the beets in a baking dish and toss them with the oil, a sprinkle each of salt and pepper, and a splash of water. Cover with foil and bake until fork tender, about 1 hour. Remove, cool enough to handle, then peel.

To serve, cut baby beets in half or cut regular beet halves in half again. Transfer to a bowl and toss with the vinegar. Add the yogurt and dill and toss to mix. Serve right away or chilled.

Cauliflower Stew with Tomato, Black Olives, and Parsley

This vegetable stew, or plaki, can also be made with any of the vegetables listed in the box on page 143. Briefly pre-soaking the cauliflower helps keep it bright and fresh-tasting as it stews to perfection.

Serves 6 to 8

1 head (about 1½ pounds) cauliflower cut into florets

2 tablespoons freshly squeezed lemon juice

1 teaspoon kosher salt

2 tablespoons extra virgin olive oil

2 medium tomatoes, peeled, seeded, and coarsely chopped

Kosher salt, to taste

⅔ cup Kalamata olives, pitted

2 tablespoons freshly squeezed lemon juice

¼ cup chopped fresh flat-leaf parsley

Place the cauliflower florets in a large bowl. Add the lemon juice, salt, and water to cover. Set aside at room temperature to soak for 30 minutes.

To cook, heat the oil in a large pot over medium heat until beginning to sizzle. Add the tomatoes and a pinch of salt and cook for 2 minutes, until the tomatoes wilt. Drain the cauliflower and add it to the pot, along with 1 cup of water. Bring to a boil over medium-high heat and cook for 5 minutes, until the cauliflower can be pierced all the way through but is still a little crisp. Transfer to a bowl and stir in the olives, lemon juice, parsley, and salt to taste. Serve right away or at room temperature.

New World Okra Stew with Tomatoes, Potatoes, and Corn

🐚 Serves 4

Tomatoes and potatoes, native to the Americas, combine with okra, native to Africa and Asia, in an Old World, plaki-style vegetable stew. With the addition of corn, the dish is transformed into a distinctly New World interpretation. Saffron, not common in Armenian cooking though not unheard of either, lends fragrance and elegance to the look of the dish.

1 pound small (2 to 2½ inches long) fresh
    okra pods

1½ teaspoons kosher salt

1 tablespoon cider vinegar

2 tablespoons butter

1 small yellow or white onion, chopped

2 medium tomatoes, coarsely chopped

½ teaspoon ground cumin

Large pinch saffron threads

½ teaspoon Aleppo pepper

Small pinch cayenne pepper

2 medium red or white potatoes, scrubbed and
    cut into ½-inch dice

1 cup water

¾ cup fresh corn kernels, cut from 1 medium
    ear of corn

1 tablespoon chopped cilantro leaves

6 lemon wedges, for serving

To prepare the okra, slice off the stems without cutting into the pods. Place the pods in a bowl, toss with 1 teaspoon of the salt and the vinegar, and set aside for 30 minutes, or up to 1 hour.

To make the stew, melt the butter in a large, heavy pot over medium-high heat. Add the onion and sauté until beginning to wilt, 3 minutes. Add the tomatoes and continue cooking until they soften and render their juices, about 5 minutes. Stir in the cumin, saffron, Aleppo pepper, cayenne pepper, potatoes, okra (without rinsing), and water. Bring to a boil over high heat, cover the pot, and simmer for 30 minutes, until the okra is tender but not soft.

Stir in the corn and cilantro and continue simmering, uncovered, for 3 minutes more, until the corn is no longer raw. Serve right away, with the lemon wedges on the side.

Armenian Ratatouille

In the tradition of long-cooked mixed-vegetable stews, this one is slow-baked so the vegetables soften and meld into each other, ratatouille-style, without frying and stirring. It's a sublime intermeshing to serve hot or cold, alongside roasts, simply grilled meats or poultry, or in Aram Sandwiches (page 65).

Serves 6 to 8

> 1 small (¾-pound) eggplant, cut into 2-inch cubes
> 2 teaspoons kosher salt
> ½ large green bell pepper, cut into 1-inch squares
> 2 medium tomatoes, cut into 6 wedges each
> 2 medium zucchini, trimmed and cut into 1-inch rounds
> 1 medium yellow or white onion, quartered and
>   sliced 1 inch thick
> 2 large cloves garlic, coarsely chopped
> ¼ cup extra virgin olive oil
> 1½ teaspoons chopped fresh marjoram or ¾ teaspoon
>   dried marjoram
> 2 teaspoons paprika, hot or mild
> 2 tablespoons chopped fresh flat-leaf parsley

Preheat the oven to 375°F.

To prepare the eggplant, place the cubes in a bowl and toss with 1½ teaspoons of the salt. Set aside for 20 to 30 minutes.

In a large oven-proof casserole dish, combine the eggplant with the bell pepper, tomatoes, zucchini, onion, garlic, oil, marjoram, paprika, and remaining ½ teaspoon salt. Gently stir to mix, cover, and bake for 1 hour, until the vegetables are meltingly soft.

Garnish with the parsley, and serve hot or cold. Will keep in the refrigerator for up to 5 days.

Stuffed Vegetables
Dolmas

Stuffed vegetables, called dolmas, were a routine dinner when I was growing up.
We usually had them as a trio offering of stuffed bell peppers, zucchini, and toma-
toes. The stuffing was always with meat, and the meat was always lamb. More
recently, I have become enamored of using meat stuffing for the bell peppers and
tomatoes, and rice stuffing for the zucchini. You can suit yourself with the following
recipes, which present variations on this very easy family food.

Serves 6

    3 medium zucchini, halved lengthwise, centers
        scooped out and reserved
    4 medium tomatoes, capped, centers scooped out,
        caps and centers reserved
    3 medium green, red, or yellow bell peppers, or a
        mixture, capped, seeds and membranes removed,
        caps reserved
    Kosher salt and freshly ground black pepper
    Basic Meat Stuffing (page 230) or Basic Rice Stuffing
        (page 231)

Preheat the oven to 350°F.

Spread the zucchini and tomato centers in the bottom of a baking dish large enough to hold all the vegetables in a single layer. Sprinkle generously with salt and pepper. Fill the vegetables with the stuffing without packing too tightly, so there is room for it to expand during cooking without bursting out of the vegetables. Place the stuffed vegetables in the casserole dish. Replace the caps on the tomatoes and peppers, and cover the dish.

Place in the oven and bake until the zucchini and tomato bed is bubbling and the vegetables are soft, 45 minutes to 1 hour, depending on the size of the vegetables. Serve right away.

BASIC MEAT STUFFING FOR DOLMAS

The ratio of meat to rice for dolma stuffing varies wildly from cook to cook, as do the seasonings. I like to balance the meat and rice 1:1 (when the rice is cooked) and zestily season it.

Makes enough for 8 medium tomatoes, 8 medium bell peppers, or 8 large squash halves

1 cup cooked long grain white rice (page 231)

½ pound ground lamb or beef

1 medium yellow or white onion, finely chopped

2 teaspoons chopped fresh oregano

½ cup chopped fresh flat-leaf parsley

1½ teaspoons kosher salt

¾ teaspoon freshly ground black pepper

¼ cup tomato paste

1 tablespoon freshly squeezed lemon juice

Place all the ingredients in a bowl and knead with your hands to mix. Use right away, or cover and refrigerate for up to 48 hours before using.

✦

BASIC RICE STUFFING FOR DOLMAS

Herbaceous and grain-good, this stuffing is suitable for any vegetarian dolma or meatless grape leaf sarma.

Makes enough for 8 medium tomatoes, 8 medium bell peppers, 8 large zucchini halves, or 65 grape leaf sarmas

1½ cups long grain white rice

3 cups water

¼ cup extra virgin olive oil

1 large onion, finely chopped

⅓ cup currants

⅓ cup pine nuts

1 tablespoon finely chopped lemon zest

2 tablespoons chopped fresh dill leaves

¼ cup chopped fresh flat-leaf parsley leaves

1 teaspoon kosher salt

½ teaspoon freshly ground black pepper

To prepare the rice, place it in a medium pot, add the water, and bring to a boil over high heat. Decrease the heat to maintain the barest simmer, cover, and cook for 22 minutes, until the grains are tender. Remove from the heat and set aside to cool and steam dry for 30 minutes or up to several hours. Transfer to a large bowl and set aside.

To make the stuffing, heat the oil in a sauté pan over medium-high heat. Add the onion, currants, and pine nuts, stir to mix, and cook until the onion is transparent, about 5 minutes. Remove from the heat and stir in the remaining ingredients. Add to the bowl with the rice and gently stir to mix. Use right away, or set aside at room temperature for up to 4 hours. The stuffing is best if not refrigerated.

Tomato Dolmas on a Potato Bed with Breadcrumb Topping

Serves 4

Tomato dolmas baked on a bed of potatoes is a satisfying, filling, and delicious home dish. I prefer the meat stuffing, made with beef, but the meatless stuffing works as well for a vegetarian dish.

> 4 large (10- to 12-ounce) ripe red tomatoes
> Kosher salt
> 1½ teaspoons freshly squeezed lemon juice
> 1 large russet potato, scrubbed and cut into ¼-inch-
>   thick slices
> ½ teaspoon freshly ground black pepper
> ½ recipe Basic Meat Stuffing (page 230), made with
>   beef, or Basic Rice Stuffing (page 231)
> 1 tablespoon extra virgin olive oil
> ¼ cup white wine
> Toasted Breadcrumb Topping (page 210)
> 1 cup yogurt, stirred smooth, for serving

If cooking in the oven, preheat it to 350°F.

To prepare the tomatoes, cut about ⅓ inch of the caps off the tomatoes and set them aside. With a spoon or paring knife, ream out the pulp, leaving the tomatoes intact. Reserve the pulp. Sprinkle the inside of the tomatoes with salt and the lemon juice.

Arrange the potato slices in the bottom of an oven casserole or microwave bowl large enough to hold the tomatoes in one layer. Sprinkle with the pepper and a liberal measure of salt. Spread the reserved tomato pulp over the potatoes. Fill the tomatoes with the stuffing you are using, set them on top of the potato bed, and cover with their caps. Pour the oil and wine into the dish, around, not into, the tomatoes.

To cook in the oven, cover the dish and bake for 1 hour, until the potatoes are fork-tender and the tomatoes are soft.

To cook in the microwave, cover and microwave on high for 20 minutes, until the potatoes are fork-tender and the tomatoes are soft.

Either way, remove and set aside for 5 minutes, until cool enough to handle.

To serve, lift off the tomato caps. Top each tomato with some of the toasted breadcrumbs, then replace the caps at a jaunty, skewed angle. Serve right away.

Eggplant Dolmas

These are amusingly called eggplant "slippers" or "shoes," depending on the size of the eggplants—slippers for the smaller, more narrow ones, and shoes for the wider, larger ones. They are a little different from regular dolmas in that the pulp of the vegetable becomes part of the stuffing.

Serves 4 to 6

1 large or 2 small (1½ pounds altogether) eggplants
⅓ cup extra virgin olive oil
1 medium yellow or white onion, finely chopped
2 large cloves garlic, finely chopped
½ cup walnuts, coarsely chopped
½ pound lean ground beef
2 tablespoons tomato paste
¼ teaspoon ground allspice
1½ teaspoons kosher salt
½ teaspoon freshly ground black pepper
½ cup red wine
¾ cup water

Cut the eggplant in half lengthwise. Scoop out the center of each half, leaving ½ inch of pulp intact. Set the shell aside. Coarsely chop the pulp and set it aside separately.

Heat the olive oil in a large sauté pan over medium-high heat. Place the shells, cut sides down, in the pan and cook until well-wilted and golden, about 10 minutes. Turn the shells over and continue cooking until browned on the skin side, about 1 minute more. Transfer, cut sides up, to a baking dish large enough to hold them in one tight layer and set aside.

To make the filling, add the onion, garlic, and walnuts to the same pan and cook over medium heat for 5 minutes, until the onion wilts. Add the meat and cook, stirring to break up the chunks, until the meat is browned, about 2 minutes. Stir in the eggplant pulp, tomato paste, allspice, salt, pepper, and wine and bring to a boil. Cover, decrease the heat to maintain a simmer, and cook for 20 minutes, until the juices are deep reddish-brown and bubbling up from the bottom of the pan. Stir in the water, cover again, and continue cooking for 10 minutes more. Remove from the heat and set aside while the oven preheats, or up to several hours.

When ready to cook, preheat the oven to 350°F.

Fill the eggplant shells with the meat mixture and pour enough water around, not into, the shells to reach ¼ inch up the sides of the dish. Place in the oven and bake for 1 hour, until the shells are tender and the filling is bubbling in the center. Remove and cool enough to handle. Serve right away or at room temperature. Or, cool and refrigerate for up to 5 days, or freeze for up to 2 weeks.

Quince or Tart Apple Dolmas
with Pork Stuffing

Serves 4 to 8

Caucasian and Middle-Eastern Armenian cooks, among many others around the Caspian, Black, Aegean, and Mediterranean seas, distinguish themselves with multitudinous meat and fruit combinations. Based on those, Susanna Hoffman and I developed this novel (because of the pork) variation when we were coauthoring our Well-Filled Microwave Cookbook. *It's one I look forward to preparing in late fall to early winter, when quinces are available and a pork and chestnut stuffing suits the season and quinces' taste. For ease, I use already-peeled, freeze-dried chestnuts, but never canned chestnuts—they have no flavor. The stuffing also works well for cabbage leaf sarmas, roast chicken, or turkey.*

Stuffing

½ pound ground pork
½ cup freeze-dried chestnuts, coarsely chopped
½ cup cooked long grain white rice (page 231)
½ medium yellow or white onion, finely chopped
½ cup chopped fresh flat-leaf parsley leaves
Small pinch of allspice
½ teaspoon kosher salt
¼ teaspoon freshly ground black pepper

4 medium quinces or large tart apples, such as
    pippins or Granny Smiths
2- to 3-inch piece cinnamon stick
1 cup water
1½ tablespoons freshly squeezed lemon juice

To make the stuffing, combine all the ingredients in a bowl and mix thoroughly.

To prepare the quinces, cut them in half lengthwise. Remove and discard the seeds and cores. Scoop out about ¼ cup of the pulp from each half (a melon baller or grapefruit spoon works best). Place the pulp, cinnamon, water, and lemon juice in a heavy pot or microwave dish large enough to hold the quince halves in one tight layer. Fill the centers of the quince with the stuffing and place them in the pot in one layer.

To cook on the stove top: Bring to a boil over medium-high heat, cover the pot, and decrease the heat to maintain a brisk simmer. Cook until the quinces are soft, 40 to 50 minutes.

To cook in the microwave: Cover the dish and microwave on high for 25 minutes, until the quinces are soft. Remove and let stand for 5 minutes.

To serve, transfer the quince halves to a platter. Remove the cinnamon stick and spoon the pulp and juices over the dolmas. Serve right away or at room temperature.

Grape Leaf Sarmas
Yalanchi

On the occasions when my traveling family reunited with the Armenian clan in Sacramento, the table was a banquet of delights and the sarmas were my favorite, beyond the shish kebab and jajik, and even the baklava. The picture of my grandmother sitting at the head of her well-filled table, and my Aunt Rose (see box, page 240) rolling dozens of grape leaves, and the cooking smells that only grape leaf sarmas have, are part of me. I still think of them as the queen dish of Armenian cooking—to the extent that I have planted two Thompson Seedless grapevines in my Oakland backyard, mostly for the leaves to make sarmas.

Makes 60 to 70 sarmas

> 60 to 70 prepared grape leaves (see box, page 239)
> 1 recipe Traditional Lamb and Rice Stuffing (page 241)
>   or Nouvelle Rice, Wild Rice, Dried Fruit, and
>   Nut Stuffing (page 241)
> Extra virgin olive oil, for serving
> 1 lemon, cut into very thin wedges

Working in batches, spread the grape leaves, veined-side up, on a counter and cut off the stems. Place a teaspoon or so, depending on the size of the leaf, near the stem end. Fold each bottom side of the leaf over the filling and roll up the leaf to make a neat cylinder. Tuck in the sides to make a package. Transfer, seam sides down, to a large heavy pot as you go, packing the cylinders tightly together and building up a layer or two, depending on the size of the pot.

Add water barely to cover and place a plate that fits inside the pot over the sarmas to keep them submerged as they cook. Bring to a boil over medium heat, cover the pot, and simmer on medium-low heat for 10 minutes. Remove from the heat and set aside to cool and finish cooking for 20 minutes.

Remove the cover and carefully pour off the water, lightly pressing down on the plate to extract as much water as you can. At this point, sarmas may be served warm (the preferred Armenian way for meat-filled sarmas) or chilled for up to 3 days.

To serve, arrange the sarmas on a platter. Moisten with a little olive oil and garnish with lemon wedges.

PREPARING GRAPE LEAVES

If you have fresh, young grape leaves (the end-of-season, older ones are too tough for sarmas, see page 222 for what to do with them), cook them in heavily salted, boiling water for 5 minutes, until softened and no longer bright green. Cool, then use right away or refrigerate in the saltwater brine for up to 2 months. If you don't have fresh grape leaves, jarred, already brined grape leaves are also fine. California-grown or kosher ones are best. Those imported from Greece have good flavor but tend to shred when rolling, so they're very difficult to work with, and those that come under various fancy food labels don't have much flavor at all.

Fresh or jarred, to prepare grape leaves for filling, drain and rinse them briefly. Fresh grape leaves may not need to have the stems trimmed off since they can be harvested without the stems attached. Jarred grape leaves usually come in rolls of overlapping leaves with a bit of stem intact. Open out the roll to expose the undersides with stems and then, without separating the leaves, cut off the stems in one fell swoop with scissors or a sharp paring knife.

CATCHING UP OVER GRAPE LEAVES

When I was in college at the University of California, Berkeley, I visited Aunt Rose during spring break, ostensibly for a few days' quiet study, but my real goal, I suspect, was to enjoy some homemade sarmas. She thought the visit was for a grand chat to cover years of family history. She made the sarmas while we talked, explaining all the while that she just didn't do this much anymore, too much trouble. . . . Of course, for an Armenian, a simple few rolled grape leaves doesn't mean anything; it has to be a tall pot full. We dined on sarmas, chatted some more, and I went back to my college room to cram for the exams.

MOCK SARMA

For an easy, and lovely, buffet party dish, arrange brined grape leaves (see box, page 239) in an overlapping layer on a large platter. Mound Tabbouli (page 100) over the leaves. Drizzle a little olive oil over the top to moisten, and decorate with black olives. Serve, letting the guests wrap up their own grape-leaf sarmas.

TRADITIONAL LAMB AND RICE
STUFFING FOR GRAPE LEAF SARMAS

*Cooking the rice before mixing it into the stuffing is a way to shorten the cooking
time for the sarmas and also to avoid having to check a sarma in the hot pot to see
if the rice is done yet. It's not traditional, but expeditious.*

Makes
enough to fill
60 to 70
grape leaves

> 1¼ cups cooked long grain white rice (page 231),
>   at room temperature
> 1 medium yellow or white onion, finely chopped
> 1 pound lean ground lamb
> ½ packed cup chopped fresh flat-leaf parsley
> 6 tablespoons tomato paste
> 3 tablespoons freshly squeezed lemon juice
> 1½ teaspoons kosher salt
> 1 teaspoon freshly ground black pepper

Combine the ingredients in a bowl, kneading lightly with your hands to
mix thoroughly. Use right away or store in the refrigerator overnight.

✤

Nouvelle Rice, Wild Rice, Dried Fruit, and Nut Stuffing for Grape Leaf Sarmas

Borrowing on my Armenian heritage, which I didn't even realize at the time, I made up this sarma stuffing with wild rice in addition to the traditional white rice for my Pig-by-the-Tail delicatessen in 1982.

Note: Plain wild rice is cooked the same way as plain white rice (page 231), except it takes longer, 35–45 minutes. When the grains are tender and open, drain any remaining water and proceed with the recipe.

Makes enough for 60 to 65 grape leaves

2 tablespoons butter

½ cup slivered almonds, finely chopped

6 sun-dried apricot halves, finely chopped

¼ cup currants

¼ cup golden raisins

1 cup cooked long grain white rice (page 231)

1 cup cooked wild rice (see Note, above)

1 large yellow or white onion, finely chopped

½ cup chopped fresh flat-leaf parsley

⅓ cup chopped fresh mint leaves

1 tablespoon finely chopped lemon rind

¼ cup freshly squeezed lemon juice

½ cup extra virgin olive oil

1 teaspoon kosher salt

Melt the butter in a sauté pan over medium-high heat. Add the almonds and stir until beginning to turn golden, about 1 minute. Add the apricots, currants, and raisins and sauté until beginning to soften, about 2 minutes. Transfer to a large bowl.

Add the remaining ingredients and stir to mix. Use right away, set aside at room temperature for up to 3 hours, or cover and refrigerate overnight.

Caucasus-Style Cabbage Sarmas with Beef and Blanched Onion Stuffing and Tomato Caper Sauce

With the sauce, these unpretentious cabbage rolls metamorphose into company fare. Without the sauce, a dollop of yogurt or Armenian Crème Fraîche (page 26) garnishes them in worthy style. Best of all, use both the sauce and the dairy. Blanching the onion tempers its pungence and softens it with no added fat.

Makes 12 sarmas, serves 4 to 6

Stuffing

1 large yellow or white onion, chopped, not too finely

¾ pound lean ground beef

2 teaspoons chopped fresh mint

¼ teaspoon allspice

½ teaspoon Aleppo pepper

1½ teaspoons kosher salt

1 large green or Savoy cabbage (about 2 pounds)

2 tablespoons butter

Kosher salt

½ cup water

2 tablespoons freshly squeezed lemon juice

Recipe continues on next page

Tomato Caper Sauce

2 tablespoons butter

2 medium tomatoes, peeled, seeded, and coarsely
    chopped

2 large cloves garlic, coarsely chopped

2 tablespoons capers, rinsed

1 teaspoon finely chopped lemon zest

¼ teaspoon Aleppo pepper

½ teaspoon kosher salt

½ cup Armenian Crème Fraîche (page 26) or yogurt,
    for serving (optional)

To make the stuffing, bring a small pot of water to boil over high heat. Add the onion and blanch for 1 minute. Drain, shake off excess liquid, and transfer to a bowl. Add the remaining ingredients and mix well. Use right away, set aside at room temperature for up to 1 hour, or refrigerate for up to 2 days.

To prepare the cabbage, bring a large pot of salted water to boil. Core the bottom of the cabbage with a paring knife. Place the cabbage in the pot, return to a boil, and cook briskly for 10 minutes, until the outer leaves are soft. Drain and set aside until cool enough to handle.

Gently pry off 14 of the outermost leaves, taking care to keep them whole. Make a **V**-cut around the remaining core in 12 of the outer leaves and remove it. Coarsely chop the remaining inner leaves, along with the core trim, and set aside.

To make the sarmas, spread about 2 tablespoons of the stuffing in the center of each cabbage leaf and roll it up to enclose the stuffing in a neat packet. (Use toothpicks to secure the rolls if necessary.) Set aside.

To cook the sarmas, melt the butter in a large, heavy pot over medium-high heat. Add the chopped cabbage, a big pinch of salt, and the water and stir to mix. Place the sarmas, seam side down, in the pot. Sprinkle salt and the lemon juice over the top and cover with the remaining 2 leaves. Bring to a boil over high heat, cover, decrease the heat to maintain a simmer, and cook for 25 minutes, until the leaves are very tender. Remove the pot from the heat and let cool for 5 minutes or so while making the sauce.

To make the sauce, melt the butter in a saucepan over medium-high heat. Add the remaining ingredients and bring to a boil. Cook for 1 minute, until the tomatoes collapse. Use right away, or store in the refrigerator for up to 3 days.

To serve, transfer the cabbage rolls to a large platter. Arrange the chopped leaves from the bottom of the pot around them. Spoon the sauce over the top and serve right away, with the crème fraîche, if using.

Chard Leaf Sarmas with Rice Pilaf, Cheese, and Yogurt Béchamel Filling

In addition to tomatoes and Armenian cucumbers, chard was always part of my father's garden. He insisted, and taught me, that white-ribbed chard is the variety that's sweetest and best, and the only kind for braising into a side dish or rolling up into sarmas. To this day, I agree.

Serves 6

6 large green, white-ribbed chard leaves
1 tablespoon butter
½ medium yellow or white onion, finely chopped
2 tablespoons chopped fresh dill
Pinch of ground nutmeg
¾ teaspoon kosher salt
2 cups Basic Rice Pilaf (page 250)
¾ cup coarsely grated Muenster cheese
1 cup Yogurt Béchamel (page 27)

To prepare the chard, bring a large pot of water to boil. Making a **V**-cut, cut out the bottom of the rib of each leaf up to the tender part. Coarsely chop the ribs and set aside. Blanch the leaves in the boiling water until completely wilted, about 2 minutes. Drain and rinse with cool water. Separate the leaves and spread them on paper towels to dry.

To make the filling, melt the butter in a large sauté pan over medium heat. Add the chopped chard ribs, along with the onion, dill, nutmeg, and salt. Sauté until softened, about 3 minutes. Stir in the pilaf, ½ cup of the cheese, and ½ cup of the béchamel. Set aside.

Preheat the oven to 375°F.

246 · *The Armenian Table*

Spread the leaves on a counter, smooth side down. Place about ½ cup of the filling at the lower third of each leaf. Fold up the bottom of each leaf to cover the filling and roll up the leaves to make a neat package. Place the chard packets in a baking dish large enough to hold them in one packed layer. Spoon the remaining ½ cup of béchamel over the leaves and sprinkle the remaining cheese over the top. Bake for 20 minutes, until the topping is bubbling. Serve right away.

Pilafs

❖

A pilaf of rice or bulgur is an essential component of an Armenian dinner. Like risottos, pilafs can be simple or fancy, adorned with few or multiple embellishments, and served as either entrée or side dish. This chapter presents basic recipes for each kind of pilaf and some more involved compositions. For another, different kind of pilaf, see Wild Rice Pilaf (page 176). Here are the simple guidelines for pilaf making:

❖ For rice pilaf, long grain rice is essential. I use basmati rice because I like its nuttiness, but long grain rice from California or Carolina also works and is more the norm. For bulgur pilafs, a coarse grind is preferred, so that the granules fluff as they absorb the liquid, but the more available medium-grind bulgur will also do.

❖ The choice between broth or water for cooking depends on the other components: For basic pilafs, water is the choice. For grander compositions, broth is used to add flavor to the mix.

❖ Pilafs may be prepared early in the day, but they are best if not refrigerated. If preparing in advance, set the pot aside at room temperature, then reheat in a bowl in a microwave oven or over very low heat on the stove top.

Basic Rice Pilaf

The basic pilaf of my family was of rice with vermicelli noodles, cooked with water, not broth. Other than the simple flourishes of salt, pepper, and a pat or two of butter at the end, there were no other trimmings. It's the way I make rice pilaf still.

Serves 4 to 6 as a side dish

1½ tablespoons butter
½ cup broken-up vermicelli or angel hair pasta
1 cup long grain white rice
2 cups water
Freshly ground black pepper
Extra butter

Heat the butter in a heavy saucepan over medium-high heat until melted. Add the vermicelli and stir until beginning to turn golden, about 1½ minutes. Add the rice and continue stirring until well coated and translucent, about 2 minutes. Add the water and bring to a boil. Decrease the heat to low, cover, and simmer without lifting the lid for 20 minutes, until the rice is cooked through.

Sprinkle freshly ground black pepper over the rice and place 2 or 3 pats of butter on top. Cover again and set aside to steam dry for at least 10 minutes, or up to several hours.

When ready to eat, gently reheat if necessary. Use two forks to fluff up the rice and mix in the pepper and butter. Serve right away.

THE SIZE OF THE POT MATTERS

It's easy enough to expand a pilaf recipe to serve more, even many more, by straightforwardly multiplying the ingredients. But there's an important point to keep in mind. For pilaf, or any other rice dish, the pot should be the size to accommodate the rice and called-for liquid so that the liquid comes about $\frac{1}{2}$ inch above the grains when you start cooking. For example, a batch for 4 should be made in a smallish pot no more than 6 to 8 inches wide. To serve a crowd, you can use a larger pot, so long as it holds the rice and liquid in the same way. In other words, don't make a small batch for 4 in a large pot because the water evaporates before the rice is cooked.

Rice and Lentil Pilaf with Sautéed Chicken Liver and Scallion Topping

Serves 4

Pilaf that includes liver is popular in Armenian cuisine. Though lamb or calves' liver is more typical, I prefer chicken liver, and always save it from the giblet package that comes along with a whole chicken so that I can make this pilaf. The liver and scallions may be served as an appetizer on their own with soft Armenian Cracker Bread (see page 63) or a warm baguette.

Pilaf

¾ cup long grain white rice

½ cup dry lentils

¾ teaspoon salt

2½ cups water

½ teaspoon Aleppo pepper

1½ tablespoons butter

Topping

2 tablespoons butter

4 chicken livers

Kosher salt and freshly ground black pepper

2 scallions, white and light green part, finely chopped

Combine the rice, lentils, salt, and water in a saucepan and bring to a boil over high heat. Decrease the heat to low, cover, and simmer until the rice and lentils are tender, 20 to 22 minutes. Gently stir in the pepper, dot the top with the butter, and, without stirring again, cover and set aside for 15 minutes.

To prepare the topping, melt the butter in a small pan over medium-high heat. Add the livers, season with salt and pepper, and sauté on both sides until golden and firm but still pink in the centers, 5 to 7 minutes.

To serve, slice the livers and set atop the pilaf. Sprinkle with the scallions and serve warm.

Rice Pilaf with Shrimp, Tomato, and Cilantro

In this versatile entrée pilaf, the shrimp shells play the important roll of enriching the stock and making it extra delicious. As well as cilantro, you can use oregano, tarragon, parsley, or dill for the herb; use saffron instead of tomato paste for the color; and/or add a feta cheese topping to make an even more sumptuous dish.

Serves 4

1 pound uncooked medium shrimp, with shells and
    tails
3 cups low-sodium chicken broth
2 tablespoons butter or extra virgin olive oil
¼ cup chopped yellow or white onion
1½ cups long grain white rice
1 tablespoon tomato paste
2 tablespoons chopped fresh cilantro leaves
½ teaspoon kosher salt
¼ teaspoon Aleppo pepper
⅓ cup crumbled feta cheese, for topping (optional)

To prepare the shrimp, remove the shells, leaving the tails intact and reserving the shells. Devein the shrimp, if necessary, and set them aside in the refrigerator.

Place the shells and broth in a small saucepan and bring to a boil over high heat. Decrease the heat to maintain a brisk simmer and cook until the shells are pink, about 3 minutes. Set aside.

To make the pilaf, melt the butter in a saucepan over medium-high heat. Add the onion and rice and sauté until the rice is translucent, about

2 minutes. Strain the reserved shrimp shell broth into the pot through a fine-mesh strainer. Add the remaining ingredients, except the feta and shrimp, stir to mix, and bring to a boil over high heat. Decrease the heat to low, cover, and simmer for 22 minutes, until the rice is tender.

Turn off the heat, remove the lid, and stir in the shrimp. Cover again and let sit for 5 minutes, until the shrimp are barely pink. Serve warm, garnished with the feta cheese, if using.

Wedding Pilaf

Wedding pilaf is an impressive dish served with grilled or roast lamb on many festive occasions (see box, page 258). I always add the scallion garnish, though it is atypical, because it adds color and a welcome piquance to the elaborate fruity, nutty composition. Dried sour plums are available in produce stores and farmers' markets; dried apricots or dried pears can substitute.

Serves 6 to 8

2 tablespoons extra virgin olive oil
1 cup broken up vermicelli or angel hair pasta
1½ cups long grain white rice
3 cups low-sodium chicken broth
⅛ teaspoon ground allspice
2 teaspoons kosher salt
1 teaspoon freshly ground black pepper
2 tablespoons butter
½ cup whole blanched almonds
⅓ cup currants
⅓ cup dried sour plum halves (not prunes), quartered
2 tablespoons finely chopped scallions, white and
    light green part, for garnish (optional)

Heat the oil in a large heavy pot over medium-high heat. Add the vermicelli and stir until lightly golden, about 1½ minutes. Add the rice and continue stirring until the rice is translucent, about 2 minutes. Add the broth, allspice, salt, and pepper, stir to mix, and bring to a boil over high heat. Decrease the heat to low, cover the pot, and simmer very gently for 25 minutes, until the rice is tender but still a little moist. Turn off the heat, leaving the pot on the burner, and set the lid ajar. Leave for 10 minutes, until the moisture is gone.

In a sauté pan, melt the butter over medium-high heat. Add the almonds, currants, and dried plums to the pan and sauté until the almonds are toasted and the fruit is soft, about 5 minutes.

To serve, spread the hot pilaf on a platter and top with the nut and fruit mixture. Sprinkle with the chopped scallion, if using, and serve right away.

SPIT-ROASTED WHOLE YOUNG LAMB
TO ACCOMPANY WEDDING PILAF:
A STORY

When I married my husband, Rick Wise, on a beautiful Fourth of July in 1977, the featured menu item was whole young lamb, spit-roasted over a deep-pit charcoal fire. Our friend Willie Bishop, artist and master cook, came to the wedding site in Orinda, California, early in the day with his assistants to dig the pits—three, because there were three lambs—and set up the spit-grilling apparatuses over the pits. However, like all weddings, this one had some melodrama. The lambs had been delivered from Dal Porto Ranch in Amador County and hung in the refrigerated locker at Chez Panisse Restaurant, across the street from my Pig-by-the-Tail delicatessen, in Berkeley. On the wedding morning, I was in Orinda, preparing to look lovely and welcome everyone to the wedding. Even though it was a holiday, a health inspector showed up at the restaurant unannounced on a routine inspection and noticed the lambs didn't have an official stamp on them. Because the carcasses were so cleanly slaughtered and perfectly dressed—Frank Dal Porto had grown up raising lambs for the family table and took great pride in that part of the job—the inspector suspected he had stumbled onto evidence of an illegal slaughterhouse operation and impounded the lambs! Fortunately, my future brother-in-law, Jerry Budrick, at the time maître d' and part-owner of Chez Panisse, was on the spot preparing a roasted peacock, fastidiously refeathered after cooking, for presentation at the wedding feast. Even more fortunately, he happened to know the head inspector (maître d's have a penchant for making good connections), whom he immediately called. All was well that ended well. The head inspector arrived and released the lambs, and they were duly delivered to the wedding site. Willie had the lambs on the fire by 11:00 A.M., in plenty of time for the aroma of grilling lamb to waft through the air, wrapping around our ceremony, and by 2:30 the feast was ready.

Basic Bulgur Pilaf

Serves 4 to 6

Wheat has been cultivated in Armenia since ancient times. As bulgur—cooked, dried, and cracked wheat—it was the original cereal of pilaf, preceding rice by many centuries. Though sometimes considered less glamorous than the later arrival, bulgur is nonetheless honored for its nutritional content—it is high in protein, phosphorous, and potassium as well as calcium, iron, thiamine, and riboflavin— and beloved for its nutty, grassy flavor. It remains a basic grain for pilafs throughout the Caucasus, in the Middle East and Greece, and in my home.

> 2 tablespoons extra virgin olive oil
> 1 small yellow or white onion, halved and thinly sliced
> 1 cup medium or coarse bulgur
> 2 cups low-sodium chicken broth
> 1 teaspoon kosher salt

Heat the oil in a saucepan over medium-high heat. Add the onion and sauté until golden, about 2 minutes. Stir in the bulgur and continue cooking until the bulgur is toasted, about 2 minutes. Add the broth and salt and bring to a boil. Decrease the heat to low, cover the pot, and simmer for 25 to 30 minutes, until the liquid is mostly evaporated. Remove from the heat and let sit for 10 minutes, until fluffy and no longer moist. Serve warm.

Bulgur and Walnut Pilaf

Bulgur and walnuts go together like ducks and water, tomatoes and basil, rhubarb and strawberries, love and marriage, and much more. They're just a natural pair, age-old born companions. Together in pilaf, they serve as a side carbohydrate dish for almost any meal, or as the meal itself when amended with yogurt and a few of-ferings from the Armenian maza table.

2 tablespoons butter
⅓ cup walnuts, coarsely chopped
⅓ cup finely chopped yellow or white onion
1 cup medium or coarse bulgur
2 cups low-sodium chicken broth or water
1 teaspoon kosher salt

Melt the butter in a saucepan over medium-high heat. Add the walnuts and onion, stir to mix, and sauté, stirring, for 3 minutes, until the walnuts are lightly golden. Stir in the bulgur, decrease the heat to medium, and continue sautéing for 2 minutes, until the bulgur is lightly toasted. Add the broth and salt, stir to mix, and bring to a boil. Decrease the heat to low, cover the pot, and simmer for 25 to 30 minutes, until the liquid is mostly evaporated. Remove from the heat and let sit for 10 minutes, until fluffy and no longer moist. Serve warm.

Bulgur Pilaf with Chickpeas, Spring Onions, and Grapevine Tendrils

*Instead of spring onions, you can use scallions. Instead of grapevine tendrils, sub-
stitute pea tendrils (available in Asian markets) plus a spritz of lemon juice. This
pilaf is also good made with rice.*

Serves 4 to 6

  2 tablespoons butter
  1 spring onion, white and light green part, chopped
      (about ¼ cup)
  1 cup medium or coarse bulgur
  ½ cup cooked chickpeas (page 35)
  2 cups water
  ¼ cup chopped fresh grapevine tendrils

Melt the butter in a saucepan over medium heat. Add the onion and sauté
for 1 minute, until wilted. Stir in the bulgur and chickpeas and continue
cooking for 2 to 3 minutes, until the bulgur is lightly toasted. Add the water and bring to a boil. Decrease the heat to low, cover the pot, and simmer for 25 minutes, until the liquid is mostly evaporated. Remove from
the heat and set aside to steam-dry for 10 to 15 minutes, until no longer
moist. Stir in the grape tendrils and serve warm.

Sweets

❖

The galaxy of sweets in Armenian cuisine is a wonder to behold, and, as M.F.K. Fisher noted in remarking on Turkish desserts in particular, they are virulent. That means, no holding back on the sugar as one after another dulcet delight is assembled to end the meal. This chapter contains a selection that comes out of my childhood memory and my recent imagination, all spun together in an appreciation of the Armenian sweet tooth combined with my love of fruit.

Baklava

Baklava, or paklava, is one of those few dishes, like pizza or ice cream, that has become "owned" by the whole world. When I was young, my grandmother, Victoria Jenanyan, would begin cooking for family occasions early in the morning, making the dough and rolling it out on the dining room table with a broomstick handle into transparent sheets of fillo for the baklava. It was an awesome sight to see her well-toned arms and deft hands, so in rhythm with the rolling, turning out the most tender fillo sheets imaginable. These days, I bow to her as I purchase ready-made fillo and carry on the tradition of making baklava at home.

Makes sixteen to eighteen 1½-inch pieces

Syrup

1 cup sugar
1 cup honey
1 cup water
1 tablespoon freshly squeezed lemon juice

Filling

2 cups walnuts, finely chopped but not pulverized
½ teaspoon powdered cinnamon
3 tablespoons sugar

1 cup (2 sticks) unsalted butter, melted
24 sheets (½ pound) fillo dough

To make the syrup, combine all the ingredients in a medium saucepan. Bring to a boil and simmer briskly until thickened and reduced, about 12 minutes. Set aside at room temperature until ready to use. (The syrup should be at room temperature and still pourable when ready to use; if cooled too much, reheat slightly.)

To make the filling, in a bowl, mix together the walnuts, cinnamon, and sugar. Set aside.

Preheat the oven to 350°F. Brush the bottom and sides of a 9 × 13-inch deep baking dish with some of the butter.

To make the baklava, place a layer of fillo in the bottom of the dish, cover with another layer, and brush the top with butter. Add another layer (2 sheets), brushing the top with butter, and then another layer, brushing the top with butter, until you have a stack 6 sheets high. Spread one-third of the filling evenly over the fillo. Layer and butter another 6 sheets in the same way. Spread another third of the filling over it. Layer and butter another 6 sheets in the same way and spread with the final third of the filling, so that you wind up with three nut layers. Top the final nut layer with the remaining 6 fillo sheets, buttering every other one as above. Finally, brush the top layer of fillo with butter.

With a sharp knife, cut through all the layers down to the bottom of the dish, making 16 to 18 diamond or 1½-inch square sections. Place in the oven and bake for 20 minutes. Pour the remaining butter across the top and continue baking until pale golden and crispy, about 25 minutes. Remove and set aside for 5 minutes, until no longer sizzling.

While still warm, tilt the pan and pour off the excess butter. Pour the syrup in between the cuts and around the edges of the sections, taking care to avoid the top or else it will get soggy. Set aside at room temperature until completely cool.

To serve, lift out the pieces as outlined. Serve right away or cover and store at room temperature for up to 5 days.

VARIATIONS FOR BAKLAVA

❖ In place of the walnuts, use 2 cups pistachios or a mix of 1 cup walnuts and 1 cup blanched almonds.

❖ In place of lemon juice in the syrup, use freshly squeezed orange or tangerine juice.

❖ In addition to the lemon juice in the syrup, add a few drops of orange flower water or rose water.

My grandmother, Victoria Jenanyan, looking as staunch as she was.

Shredded Fillo Pastry with Cheese and Date Filling
Kadaif

Also called kadeyef or kadayif, this sweet pastry is made with finely shredded fillo. You can find it in Middle Eastern markets or, sometimes, in large supermarkets. If you can't find it, you can cut the more available sheet fillo into very thin, less than ¹/₁₆-inch-wide, strips.

Serves 12

Filling

    1 pound fresh, unsalted cheese, such as Homemade
        Fresh Cheese (page 48) or farmer's cheese

    2 tablespoons half-and-half cream (if using homemade
        cheese)

    1 large egg, beaten

    ½ cup pitted dates, finely chopped

    1 tablespoon finely chopped orange zest

    2 tablespoons sugar

Syrup

    ½ cup flower-scented honey

    ½ cup sugar

    ¼ cup Triple Sec or other orange liqueur

    1 pound shredded fillo

    1 cup (2 sticks) butter, melted

To make the filling, mix together the cheese, half-and-half, if using home-made cheese, egg, dates, zest, and sugar. Set aside.

To make the syrup, combine the honey, sugar, and liqueur in a small saucepan and bring to a boil over medium-high heat. Stir to mix and boil for 3 minutes. Remove and set aside.

Preheat the oven to 350°F.

Spread out the shredded fillo on a counter and pull the strands apart with your fingers to separate them somewhat. Place half the strands in an 8 × 10-inch baking dish and toss with half the butter. Press down firmly to make an even crust. Spread the filling over the top. Add the remaining half of the fillo strands and pour the remaining butter over the top. Press down again to flatten and compact the layers. Place in the oven and bake until golden, about 45 minutes. Remove and let cool for about 10 minutes.

Pour the syrup over the pastry. Let stand for at least 15 minutes, up to several hours, for the syrup to be absorbed. Will keep at room temperature, loosely covered with plastic wrap, for 3 days.

To serve, cut into approximately 2 × 3-inch squares.

VARIATIONS FOR KADAIF

❖ Right after pouring on the syrup, sprinkle finely chopped pistachio nuts over the top.

❖ Instead of the cheese and date filling, use the nut filling for baklava, (page 264) or one of its variations (page 266).

Armenian Shortbread Cookies
Kurabia

Makes 30
cookies

My mother always made a version of these Armenian shortbread cookies for Christmas. She called them "dream bars" and made dozens upon dozens so that we could have our fill, with plenty more to give to the neighbors and shopkeepers for holiday treats. Kurabia remain the cookie of my dreams, and I offer a basic recipe, with a filling, which my mother didn't use, and many variations because they are so adaptable to the whim of the cook.

Filling

½ cup finely chopped walnuts

2 tablespoons raw sugar

⅛ teaspoon ground cinnamon

1 egg white, beaten (see Recipe Notes, page 271)

Cookies

½ cup vegetable shortening, at room temperature
    (see Recipe Notes, page 271)

½ cup (1 stick) butter, at room temperature

¾ cup superfine sugar

2 cups all-purpose flour

To make the filling, combine the walnuts, sugar, and cinnamon in a small bowl. Stir in the egg white and set aside.

Preheat the oven to 300°F.

In a large bowl, cream the shortening, butter, and sugar together until light and fluffy. Add the flour and beat until thoroughly mixed (dough will appear crumbly).

Gather up the dough and press it into a smooth ball. Pinch off walnut-size pieces of the dough and roll each between the palms of your hands. Set the balls on ungreased baking sheets about 2 inches apart.

Make an indentation in the top of each ball and fill with about ½ teaspoon of the filling. Bake for 25 minutes, until set but still soft. (Don't overcook; cookies should not brown.) Remove and let cool completely on the baking sheets before serving. The cookies are best if left to rest overnight; they will keep in an airtight tin for up to 2 weeks.

VARIATIONS FOR KURABIA

Kurabia invite imaginative variations. Here are some of the best.

❖ Add 1 tablespoon whiskey or brandy, 1 teaspoon almond extract, or ½ teaspoon orange flower water or rose water to the dough.

❖ Add 1 teaspoon finely chopped orange zest to the dough.

❖ Instead of walnuts, use almonds, pistachios, pine nuts, or hazelnuts for the filling.

❖ Instead of using the filling, incorporate the chopped nuts into the dough.

❖ After filling, pinch the cookies into an egg shape, enclosing the filling. These are called Easter kurabia.

❖ Add 1 teaspoon almond extract to the dough and instead of the filling, press a whole blanched almond in the center of each cookie.

❖ Sift confectioners' sugar over the cookies after baking, while they are still warm.

RECIPE NOTES

✦ Kurabia are sometimes made with all shortening, sometimes with all butter, sometimes with half shortening and half butter. The latter is what I prefer because the shortening helps make the cookies tender without being too rich; they are supposed to be delicate. I strongly recommend an organic shortening with no palm or coconut oil or trans fats, available in health food stores.

✦ For tenderness, also, use superfine sugar, which melts down more readily as the cookies bake at moderate heat.

✦ The egg white may be beaten in a blender or mini food processor. It won't form high peaks, but it will thicken and stiffen enough to do the job of binding the filling.

Peach and Cherry Pie
with Pine Nut Crust

Whenever my mother made a pie, she always rolled out the leftover dough a second time and cut it into cookies to subdue the children while we waited for the pie to be done and the dinner to get to the dessert stage. I learned this trick from her and have never tossed out those little scraps of dough. The pine nut crust dough is especially amenable to easy re-rolling without cracking or becoming tough.

 Makes one 10-inch pie and about 10 "extra cookies"

Pine Nut Crust

½ cup pine nuts

1½ cups all-purpose flour

½ teaspoon kosher salt

4 tablespoons (½ stick) cold butter, cut up

4 tablespoons cold vegetable shortening (see page 271),
  cut up

4 tablespoons water

Filling

5 ripe yellow peaches, preferably freestone for ease
  of pitting, peeled and halved (see page 288)

2 tablespoons sugar

2 teaspoons freshly squeezed lemon juice

½ pound red cherries, pitted

1 tablespoon raw sugar

To make the crust, pulverize the pine nuts in a food processor. Add the flour and salt and pulse 3 times to mix. Add the butter, shortening, and water and pulse until the mixture can be gathered into a ball. Wrap in plastic wrap, press to smooth into a thick disc, and chill for 30 minutes. Use right away or let chill longer, removing from the refrigerator 20 minutes before rolling out.

Preheat the oven to 425°F. Line a 10- to 11-inch pie pan with the dough.

Prick the crust across the bottom with a fork and place in the oven. Pre-bake for 15 minutes, until lightly golden. Remove and set aside.

Slice the peaches ¼ to ½ inch thick and toss with the sugar and lemon juice. Arrange in the pie shell, along with the cherries, and sprinkle the raw sugar over the top. Bake for 20 to 25 minutes, until the crust is dark golden and crisp. Let cool enough to handle, then slice and serve.

PINE NUT COOKIES

To make the dough into cookies, gather up the trim from lining the pie pan (or make a batch just for cookies) and roll it out about ¼ inch thick. Cut into 3-inch rounds or any other desired shape. Sprinkle the tops with raw sugar and place the cookies on a lightly greased baking sheet. Bake at 425°F for 9 to 10 minutes, until golden and crisp.

Lemon Yogurt Cake Soaked in Lemon Mint Syrup

Yogurt cake, a staple of Armenian and pan-Mediterranean desserts, is sometimes served with just a dusting of powdered sugar or, more extravagantly, doused in a honey or sugar syrup. Here is an ultimate version for those, like me, whose teeth sometimes "itch" for extra sweetness. The cake itself is a "piece of cake" to make. So is the syrup, which lends itself to aromatic variations (see pages 275–276).

 Makes one
9-inch cake

Cake

Butter for greasing the bundt pan

½ cup (1 stick) butter, at room temperature

¾ cup sugar

1 cup yogurt

2 large eggs

2 tablespoons freshly squeezed lemon juice

2 cups all-purpose flour

½ teaspoon baking soda

1 teaspoon baking powder

Lemon Mint Syrup

1 cup sugar

¼ cup freshly squeezed lemon juice

¾ cup water

3 sprigs mint

Preheat the oven to 350°F. Lightly grease a 9-inch bundt or tube pan.

In a large bowl, cream together the butter and sugar until light and fluffy. Beat in the yogurt, then the eggs, one at a time, until well mixed. Beat in the lemon juice. Sift the flour, baking soda, and baking powder into the bowl and beat until well mixed. Spoon the batter into the prepared pan and bake until golden on top, pulling away from the edges, and a knife inserted in the center comes out clean, about 40 minutes. Remove and let cool until no longer hot, 15 to 20 minutes.

While the cake bakes and cools, make the syrup. Combine all the ingredients in a small saucepan, stir to mix and dissolve the sugar a bit, and bring to a boil over high heat. Decrease the heat to maintain a brisk boil without overflowing the pan and cook for 8 to 10 minutes, until thick enough to coat a spoon. Remove the mint sprigs and set the syrup aside until cooled to warm.

When the cake and syrup are cool, loosen the cake around the edge and center tube of the pan with a knife. Leaving the cake in the pan, pour one-third of the syrup over the cake and let sit for 10 minutes for the syrup to soak in. Repeat twice more, with another third of the syrup each time. The final time, set the cake aside at room temperature to soak in the syrup for at least 1 hour, or up to several hours.

To serve, invert the cake onto a platter (pry it loose with a kitchen knife, if necessary). Slice, and serve.

FLAVORING VARIATIONS FOR LEMON YOGURT CAKE

Like the pound or sponge cakes that are more familiar to European and American cooks, lemon yogurt cake can be considered a base for many kinds of embellishments. Besides the lemon mint syrup, here are some ways to dress the cake in style.

❖ For the syrup, instead of lemon and mint, vary the syrup flavorings with: orange flower water and some orange zest; rose water and a garnish of garden rose petals, preferably red roses; a tablespoon or so of good Scotch or bourbon.

❧ Instead of the lemon mint syrup, use the syrup from Sun-dried Apricots in Almond-scented Syrup (page 281).

❧ Instead of any syrup at all, garnish the cake with fresh blackberries, strawberries or raspberries, or a mix of them and a little Sweetened Yogurt Cheese (page 297).

❧ Instead of soaking the cake in syrup, sift confectioners' sugar over the top and sprinkle with shaved bittersweet chocolate while the cake is still warm.

Walnut Spice Cake Soaked in Orange Honey Syrup

I use a bundt pan for this Caucasian-style nut cake because the cake has more surface to soak up the syrup. The raw sugar adds a pleasing, and unusual, crunch.

 Makes one 10-inch bundt cake

Butter for greasing the bundt pan
2 tablespoons plus ¾ cup raw sugar
2 cups all-purpose flour
1 teaspoon baking soda
1 teaspoon baking powder
½ teaspoon powdered cinnamon
½ teaspoon ground cloves
½ cup (1 stick) butter, at room temperature
1 cup granulated sugar
2 large eggs
1 cup plain yogurt
1 cup walnuts, finely chopped

Orange Honey Syrup

⅓ cup freshly squeezed orange juice
¼ cup honey
1 cup sugar
⅔ cup water
1 teaspoon orange flower water

Preheat the oven to 350°F. Lightly grease a 10-inch bundt pan with butter and sprinkle the 2 tablespoons raw sugar around the bottom and sides.

Sift together the flour, baking soda, baking powder, cinnamon, and cloves. Set aside.

Cream together the butter, granulated sugar, and remaining ¾ cup raw sugar. Beat in the eggs, one at a time. Beat in the dry ingredients alternately with the yogurt, one-third at a time. Stir in the walnuts. Spoon the batter into the bundt pan and bake for 45 minutes, until a knife inserted in the center comes out clean. Remove and let cool for 15 to 20 minutes.

While the cake bakes and cools, make the syrup. Combine the orange juice, honey, sugar, and water in a small saucepan and bring to a boil over high heat. Decrease the heat to maintain a brisk simmer and cook for 8 to 10 minutes, until thick enough to coat a spoon. Remove from the heat and stir in the orange flower water. Set aside until cooled to warm.

When the cake and syrup are cool, loosen the cake around the edge and center tube with a knife, leaving the cake in the pan. Pour one-third of the syrup over the cake and let sit for 10 minutes to soak in. Repeat twice more, with another third of the syrup each time. Set the cake aside to soak in the syrup for at least 1 hour, or up to several hours.

To serve, invert the cake onto a large plate (pry it loose with a kitchen knife, if necessary). Slice, and serve.

Poppy Seed Cake with Olive and Walnut Oils

Both breadlike and cakelike, poppy seed cake leaves nothing to be desired in the sweet realm, except, perhaps, for a dollop of sweetened yogurt.

Makes one 10-inch bundt cake

Butter and flour, for preparing the bundt pan
3 cups all-purpose flour
1½ teaspoons baking soda
½ teaspoon kosher salt
1¾ cups sugar
4 large eggs
1 cup extra virgin olive oil
½ cup walnut oil
1½ cups half-and-half cream
1 cup walnuts, very finely chopped
4 tablespoons poppy seeds
1 recipe Sweetened Yogurt Cheese (page 297), for
    serving

Preheat the oven to 350°F. Lightly grease and flour a 10-inch bundt pan. Sift together the flour, baking soda, and salt. Set aside.

Cream the sugar and eggs together in a large bowl until light and fluffy. Beat in the oils. Add the flour mixture in two rounds, alternately with the half-and-half, beating well after each addition. Stir in the walnuts and poppy seeds and pour the batter into the prepared bundt pan. Bake for 1 hour and 10 minutes, until a knife inserted in the center of the cake comes out clean. Remove from the oven and let rest for 1 hour.

To serve, loosen the cake around the edge and center tube and unmold onto a plate. Cut into portions and garnish with the Sweetened Yogurt Cheese.

Sun-dried Apricots in Almond-scented Syrup

Armenians describe this as "apricot delicacy." And it is, a very sweet one, at that. Suspended in their syrup, which I like to scent with almond and brighten with lemon, the apricots make a complete treat on their own, like a Greek-style spoon sweet. Or, combine them with a little of the syrup to drape over a mound of ice cream, to top scones, or garnish Lemon Yogurt Cake (page 274).

Makes about 3 cups

1 pound dried apricot halves
2 cups water
¼ cup freshly squeezed lemon juice
1½ cups sugar
1 teaspoon almond extract

Place all the ingredients except the almond extract in a heavy saucepan large enough to hold the apricots in one slightly overlapping layer. Bring to a boil over medium heat and cook until the apricots are completely soft and the liquid is thick and golden, about 10 minutes. Stir in the almond extract and set aside to cool.

Use right away or transfer to a storage container and refrigerate for up to several months.

Sun-dried Apricot Halves with Sweet Cheese and Pistachio Nut Dust

Makes 36 filled apricot halves

With a jazzy name and carnival look, these delightful tidbits are a sure conversation opener, and the taste consistently satisfies anyone looking for a sweet bite at the buffet table.

Note: The apricots may be filled with the cheese, covered with plastic wrap, and refrigerated for up to 2 days. Sprinkle on the pistachio dust just before serving.

½ cup shelled pistachio nuts
36 Sun-dried Apricots in Almond-scented Syrup
    (page 281)
1½ cups Homemade Fresh Cheese (page 48) or
    Sweetened Yogurt Cheese (page 297)
1 tablespoon confectioners' sugar, if using homemade
    cheese

Spread the pistachio nuts in a heavy skillet or on a microwave plate. Toast over high heat, stirring, or microwave on high until golden, 3 to 4 minutes either way. Transfer to a food processor and finely chop until dustlike. Set aside.

Lift the apricot halves out of the syrup and place them, open-side up, in one layer on two plates or a large platter. If using homemade cheese, stir the sugar into it. Fill each apricot half with about ½ tablespoon of the cheese. Drizzle a little of the syrup over each half and sprinkle some pistachio "dust" over the top. Serve right away or keep for up to 2 days as described in the note above.

Fresh Figs Poached in Zinfandel with Zinfandel Ice and Kaymak Cream

🍒 Serves 6

Earthy, dense, heady, and big-fruited Zinfandel evokes the taste of ancient Armenian wine in my imagination. With figs poached in it, accompanied with a New World zinfandel ice, garnished with a knob of thick, Armenian-style cooked cream, you have a splendiferous sweet plate.

Zinfandel Ice

    1 750-ml bottle zinfandel wine
    2 cups sugar
    1 tablespoon freshly squeezed lemon juice

Figs

    1 cup sugar
    1 cup water
    2 cups zinfandel wine
    1½ pounds firm, ripe Mission or other dark fresh figs

    ¾ cup Kaymak (page 296), for serving

To make the ice, stir together the wine, sugar, and lemon juice in a heavy saucepan over medium-high heat. Bring to a boil, decrease the heat to maintain a simmer, and cook for 15 minutes, until beginning to thicken.

Remove and cool completely, then transfer to a glass or heavy plastic container and place in the freezer for 2 hours, until ice crystals begin to form around the edges and across the top. Whisk to break up and mix in the ice crystals and return to the freezer for 2 hours more. Whisk again, breaking up the crystals and making an evenly granulated mixture. Cover with plastic wrap and return to the freezer until frozen through, 2 to 3 hours, or up to several days.

To poach the figs, combine the sugar, water, and wine in a large, heavy saucepan and stir to mix and dissolve the sugar a bit. Set over medium-high heat and bring to a boil. Add the figs, decrease the heat to maintain a simmer, and cook for 10 minutes, until the figs are wrinkled and slightly soft but maintain their shape. Remove from the heat and let the figs cool in the liquid. Refrigerate until chilled, at least 2 hours, or up to 2 days.

To serve, place 2 of the poached figs on each of 6 high-lip plates or wide bowls. Spoon some of the poaching liquid over and around them. Set a small scoop of the ice to one side of the figs and top it with a small scoop of kaymak. Serve right away.

Yogurt Panna Cotta with Cherry Sauce

In my interest to expand yogurt horizons as far as possible, for this volume I made a panna cotta, the delightful Italian molded custard of sugar and cream set with gelatin, based on it. What better to top it with than a sauce of one of Armenia's beloved fruits, cherries. The cherry sauce can be used to top ice cream, cake, muffins, waffles, or pancakes.

Makes four 1-cup custards

Panna Cotta

1 teaspoon powdered gelatin

1 tablespoon hot water

½ cup heavy cream

¼ cup sugar

1 cup yogurt, whisked smooth

½ teaspoon almond extract

Cherry Sauce

1 pound cherries, pitted

½ cup sugar

¼ cup kirsch

1 tablespoon freshly squeezed lemon juice

To make the panna cotta, combine the gelatin and water in a small bowl and set aside for 5 minutes, until the gelatin softens. Combine the cream and sugar in a saucepan over medium heat and, stirring constantly, bring almost to a boil, about 1 minute. Remove from the heat and stir in the gelatin mixture, whisking to smooth. Set aside to cool for 15 minutes.

Whisk in the yogurt and almond extract and pour the mixture into 4 small custard cups. Cover each cup with plastic wrap and place in the refrigerator to chill and set, at least 4 hours, or up to overnight.

To make the cherry sauce, place all the ingredients in a heavy saucepan, stir to mix, and bring to a boil over medium-high heat. Decrease the heat to medium low and simmer gently for 30 minutes, until the cherries completely collapse and the liquid is thick and syrupy. Remove from the heat and set aside to cool. When cool, transfer to a storage container and chill before serving. Will keep in the refrigerator for several weeks.

To serve, unmold the panna cotta onto 4 serving dishes. Spoon some of the cherry sauce over each plate and serve right away.

My Mother's Put-by Peaches

My mother made perfect tourshi and other savory Armenian pickles, but her preserved peaches were her biggest claim to fame. Not cooked, they were simply covered in a light sugar syrup, sealed, and stored for winter days. Orange-fleshed freestone O'Henrys were the variety of choice—perhaps because my father's name was Henry, and also because they are one of the most ambrosial of peaches. The first jar was always opened for his birthday at the end of November, and the peaches were sliced to top a thirteen–egg white angel food cake. On other days, my mother served these as halves, each moistened with some of the syrup. They are equally divine cut up and spooned over ice cream, morning cereal, or Tarkana Pudding (page 293).

I always add pomegranate molasses to the syrup and, sometimes, whole spices, such as allspice berries, cardamom seeds, whole cloves, or coriander seeds. Today, I don't seal the jars in a water bath, preferring the less time-consuming method of refrigerator storage.

Makes
4 quarts
peaches

Syrup

3 cups sugar

5 cups water

2 tablespoons pomegranate molasses

12 freestone peaches (6 to 7 ounces each), such as
    O'Henrys or Babcocks
2 whole lemons, scrubbed and cut in half

To make the syrup, combine the sugar and water in a saucepan, stir to mix, and bring to a boil over high heat. Boil for 5 minutes, stirring once, until the sugar dissolves and the mixture is slightly thickened. Remove from the heat, stir in the pomegranate molasses, and set aside to cool completely.

While the syrup cools, bring a pot of water large enough to hold the peaches in one layer to a boil over high heat. Ever so gently drop in the peaches, leave to the count of 20, and gently drain. Set aside until cool enough to handle.

With your fingers, slip the skins off the peaches. Pare away any bruised or soft spots, then cut the peaches in half around the "seam." Twist the halves in opposite directions to release the pits, and discard the pits. Pack the halves into quart jars. Pour in the completely cooled syrup, filling to the top. Set a lemon half on top (to keep the peaches submerged) and cap the jars. Refrigerate for 3 days before using. Will keep in the refrigerator for up to 6 months.

Three Nut Brittles

The microwave is a candy-making machine par excellence. Brittles are particularly successful, and I offer three variations that smack of Armenian deliciousness and are so easy to prepare, you might wonder why you don't just make some today, or at least for the next party. Be sure to read the safety guidelines before beginning (see page 292).

Note: Brittles need to be cooked to the hard-crack stage. There are two ways to determine this: When drops form brittle threads when dropped into cold water, or when the candy mixture registers between 290 and 310°F on a candy thermometer.

PUMPKIN SEED BRITTLE WITH VANILLA

Butter for greasing the foil
1 teaspoon vegetable or olive oil, for toasting the seeds
2 cups hulled raw pumpkin seeds
½ teaspoon kosher salt
¼ teaspoon cardamom seeds
2½ cups sugar
1 cup light corn syrup
2 tablespoons butter, cut up
¼ cup water
1 teaspoon vanilla extract
½ teaspoon baking soda

⌐◦ Makes about
1 pound

Lightly grease a 24-inch length of extra-wide, heavy-duty aluminum foil with butter. Heat the oil in a large sauté pan over medium heat. Add the pumpkin seeds and salt and cook, stirring often, until lightly toasted, about 5 minutes. Set aside.

Combine the cardamom, sugar, corn syrup, butter, and water in a 6-quart microwave bowl and microwave uncovered on high for 3 minutes, until the butter melts. Stir to mix and continue microwaving on high for 5 to 6 minutes, until bubbling briskly. Stir in the pumpkin seeds and microwave for 5 minutes more, until the hard-crack stage. Remove and whisk in the vanilla and baking soda, stirring until the bubbling stops. Immediately, and very carefully, pour the candy onto the foil. Set aside to cool and harden for at least 1 hour.

SESAME BRITTLE WITH ORANGE FLOWER WATER

Butter for greasing the foil
1½ cups white sesame seeds
¾ cup sugar
¾ cup natural raw honey
3-inch piece cinnamon stick
2 tablespoons water
½ teaspoon orange flower water
¼ teaspoon baking soda

Makes about
¼ pound

Lightly grease a 24-inch length of extra-wide, heavy-duty aluminum foil with butter. Heat a large, heavy, ungreased sauté pan over medium-high heat. Add the sesame seeds and cook, stirring constantly, until light golden and beginning to pop, 2 to 2½ minutes.

Transfer to a 6-quart microwave bowl. Add the sugar, honey, cinnamon stick, and water and stir to mix. Microwave uncovered on high for 3 minutes, until starting to boil. Stir and continue microwaving on high for 1 minute. Stir again and microwave for 3 minutes, until the hard-crack stage. Remove and whisk in the orange flower water and baking soda, stirring until the bubbling stops. Immediately, and very carefully, pour the candy onto the foil. Set aside to cool and harden for at least 1 hour.

WALNUT BRITTLE WITH ROSE WATER

Butter, for greasing the foil
Olive or vegetable oil, for toasting the nuts
2 cups coarsely chopped walnuts
2 cups sugar
1 cup natural raw honey
2 tablespoons butter, cut up
$\frac{1}{4}$ cup water
$\frac{1}{2}$ teaspoon rose water
$\frac{1}{2}$ teaspoon baking soda

Makes about
1¾ pounds

Lightly grease a 24-inch length of extra-wide, heavy-duty aluminum foil with butter. Lightly grease a large sauté pan with about 1 teaspoon of oil and heat over medium-high heat. Add the walnuts and cook, stirring often, until lightly toasted, about 3 minutes. Set aside.

Combine the sugar, honey, butter, and water in a 6-quart microwave bowl and microwave uncovered on high for 3 minutes, until the butter melts. Stir to mix and continue microwaving on high for 5 to 6 minutes, until bubbling briskly almost to the top of the bowl and starting to turn golden. Stir in the walnuts and microwave for 5 minutes more, until the hard-crack stage. Remove and whisk in the rose water and baking soda, stirring until the bubbling stops. Immediately, and very carefully, pour the candy onto the foil. Set aside to cool and harden for at least 1 hour.

SAFETY GUIDELINES FOR CANDY MAKING

❖ Use a 6-quart glass bowl so that the candy mixture doesn't boil over during cooking.

❖ Use only heavy-duty, extra-wide aluminum foil for pouring the candy onto, so the counter is protected from the heat of the candy and doesn't burn.

❖ When the candy is done, work quickly to pour it onto the foil: an extra pair of hands to scrape the candy out of the bowl as you hold it is a big help here.

❖ *Take care* to keep from touching the bowl when stirring the candy during cooking and never, ever, be tempted to take a taste before it has cooled because hot sugar will cause an *immediate* burn.

NUT BRITTLES AT THEIR BEST

Hard as it may be to resist serving and eating them right away, nut brittles are quite a lot better if allowed to "cure" for a week or so. To do so, store brittle at room temperature on its foil bottom, loosely covered with another length of foil. It will keep this way for many weeks.

Tarkana:
An Ancient Recipe

Ancient as wheat and honey, old as water, the confection called tarkana nonetheless did not reach its pinnacle of perfection until the spice routes were opened from the Far East through the Caucasus and to Armenia. That's because it is the spicing that Tarkana relies on to elevate it beyond a mere sweet into a treat. It can be served warm as a pudding, but I find it far more interesting if left to dry out into a granolalike bar—I think of it as the original power bar you can take anywhere (see page 294).

Serves 4 to 6 as a pudding or makes twelve 1 × 2-inch bars

¾ cup sugar

1 tablespoon grape syrup (see box, page 295) or
   natural raw honey

4 cups water

¾ cup cracked wheat or coarse bulgur

¼ teaspoon powdered cinnamon

¼ teaspoon ground cloves

¼ teaspoon grated nutmeg

¼ teaspoon powdered ginger

¼ teaspoon ground allspice

Optional toppings, if serving as a pudding

Chopped walnuts

My Mother's Put-by Peaches (page 287)

Armenian Crème Fraîche (page 26)

Combine the sugar, grape syrup or honey, and 1½ cups of the water in a saucepan over medium-high heat and bring to a boil. Stir to mix, add the remaining 2½ cups water and the cracked wheat, and bring to a boil again. Decrease the heat to maintain a simmer and cook until the liquid is mostly absorbed and the mixture is very thick but still moist, about 45 minutes. Stir in the spices, decrease the heat to low, and continue cooking, stirring frequently, until the mixture is almost dry, 10 to 15 minutes.

To serve, spoon into bowls and top with chopped walnuts, sliced preserved peaches, and a dollop of Armenian Crème Fraîche, if using. Or, see below for making dried tarkana bars.

TARKANA "POWER BARS"

When the tarkana is done, stir in ¾ cup chopped, toasted walnuts. Rinse an 8 × 8-inch or 9 × 5-inch metal baking pan with cold water (this is to prevent sticking). Spoon the tarkana into the pan and set aside to cool completely. Cover loosely and let sit overnight at room temperature.

The next day, preheat the oven to 300°F. Line a cookie sheet with cheesecloth. Unmold the tarkana onto a length of wax paper and cut it into 1 × 2-inch rectangles. Transfer the bars to the cookie sheet and place in the oven. Bake for 3 hours. Turn off the heat and let sit in the oven overnight.

On the third day, while the tarkana is still in the oven, preheat the oven to 250°F. Remove the tarkana once the oven reaches 250°F and transfer the bars to a large plate lined with paper towels. Cover with paper towels and let sit overnight at room temperature. Use right away. Or, loosely wrap each bar in waxed paper and store at room temperature for up to 3 weeks.

GRAPE HONEY: PEKMEZ

Called pekmez, grape honey is an exotic ingredient of Middle Eastern and Mediterranean cooking. But it's not particularly mysterious; it's simply the juice of sweet, ripe grapes that has been clarified with potash and slow-cooked until reduced to a honeylike consistency. I highly recommend its fruity sweet flavor for sweetening tarkana. You can find it in markets that cater to those cuisines, or order it online from www.kalustyans.com.

Two Armenian Dessert Cream Cheeses

Kaymak is like cream-cheese candy. Its dense texture is achieved from slowly boiling heavy cream to evaporate the water content, leaving just the toothsome butterfat. An alternative that requires no cooking, just lengthy draining, is Sweetened Yogurt Cheese (page 297). Both are used profusely in Armenian desserts to top pastries and poached fruits or to spread on toast that is then drizzled with honey. I offer both recipes below—Kaymak for the archivists among us who like to contemplate as they stir, and Sweetened Yogurt Cheese for those who prefer a less labor-intensive cream cheese.

Armenian Cream Cheese: Kaymak

1 quart heavy (whipping) cream

🍮 Makes about 2 cups

Pour the cream into a heavy saucepan, set it over medium-low heat, and bring to a boil without stirring. This will take about 45 minutes or so, depending on the width of the pan.

With a ladle, lift out some of the cream and pour it back into the pan from a height of 12 inches above the surface of the cream. This will cause bubbles to form. Repeat several times until the skin is reincorporated into the cream. Let come to a boil again, 5 to 7 minutes. Repeat the ladling process for about 45 minutes, slowly letting the milk come to a boil again each time. Scrape down the sides with a rubber spatula, ladle once more, and remove from the heat. Transfer to a rectangular dish and set aside at room temperature until the cream is set. Cover and refrigerate overnight.

With a knife, loosen around the edges of the cream with a knife, divide into 6 to 8 sections, and transfer to a plate with a metal spatula. Use right away, or wrap the sections in plastic wrap and store in the refrigerator for up to 1 week, or freeze for up to 1 month.

Sweetened Yogurt Cheese

1 quart plain yogurt, drained overnight (page 24)
1 tablespoon confectioners' sugar

Makes about
2 cups

Stir the sugar into the yogurt. Continue to drain until you have a cheese-like consistency as described on page 25. Will keep in the refrigerator for up to 2 weeks.

Turkish Coffee

Turkish coffee, served after dessert, is an essential finale to traditional Armenian meals. It is boiled rather than pressed or dripped or percolated. In this sense, it is akin to American "cowboy" coffee, which is a rapid, single boiling of the grounds in a container over a fire, but the Turkish version is more refined, and it requires a more elaborate procedure of several boilings. It also requires a very fine, pulverized grind, preferably of medium-bodied arabica beans such as are grown in Yemen, but any coffee with similar characteristics can be used successfully. Turkish coffee is invariably a sweet beverage. The somewhat acidic arabica beans cry out for sugar to soften them and make them palatable, and the sugar helps create the desirable foam. You can add more or less sweetening to taste.

Makes 8 demitasse cups

8 rounded teaspoons very finely ground coffee
8 rounded demitasse spoons (about 2 teaspoons altogether) sugar
3 cups water

Place all the ingredients in a narrow pot over medium heat (see opposite page). Stir briefly, then bring to a boil. Allow to boil for 15 seconds, until a creamy foam begins to collect on the surface. Remove from the heat long enough to stop the boiling. Return to the heat and repeat the process 4 more times. (Each time, the foam becomes thicker and increases in quantity).

Spoon the foam into 8 demitasse cups. Carefully pour the coffee into the cups without dispersing the foam and serve right away.

TURKISH COFFEE-MAKING FINESSE

❖ The very fine grind necessary for Turkish coffee can easily be achieved with a simple, revolving-blade electric coffee grinder or, more authentically, with a tall, cylindrical Turkish hand grinder that can double as a spice grinder.

❖ If you don't have an *ibek,* a Turkish coffee pot, a 1-quart saucepan will do as long as it is tall and narrow rather than wide-mouthed, so that when the coffee boils up, the desirable foamy "head" is thick and creamy.

A FINAL NOTE: HOW THINGS CHANGE

In Turkish-Armenian tradition, a festive get-together is always finished with a round of Turkish coffee and several rounds of backgammon. Traditionally, the coffee was made by the women as they cleaned up the kitchen and did the dishes while the men and older children played backgammon. These days, the men often make the coffee, the game has changed to poker—women invited, if they'd care to play—and the children often beat everyone at the game. Always, everyone helps with the dishes.

Index

❖